STILL

when all else fades away

TIFFANY NARDONI

WESTBOW
PRESS®
A DIVISION OF THOMAS NELSON
& ZONDERVAN

Scripture taken from the Holy Bible, NEW INTERNATIONAL VERSION®. Copyright © 1973, 1978, 1984, 2011 by Biblica, Inc. All rights reserved worldwide. Used by permission. NEW INTERNATIONAL VERSION® and NIV® are registered trademarks of Biblica, Inc. Use of either trademark for the offering of goods or services requires the prior written consent of Biblica US, Inc.

This book is a work of non-fiction. Unless otherwise noted, the author and the publisher make no explicit guarantees as to the accuracy of the information contained in this book and in some cases, names of people and places have been altered to protect their privacy.

Credit interior pictures: Lindy Belley
Credit cover image: Erin Caldwell

WestBow Press books may be ordered through booksellers or by contacting:

WestBow Press
A Division of Thomas Nelson & Zondervan
1663 Liberty Drive
Bloomington, IN 47403
www.westbowpress.com
1 (866) 928-1240

Because of the dynamic nature of the Internet, any web addresses or links contained in this book may have changed since publication and may no longer be valid. The views expressed in this work are solely those of the author and do not necessarily reflect the views of the publisher, and the publisher hereby disclaims any responsibility for them.

Any people depicted in stock imagery provided by Thinkstock are models, and such images are being used for illustrative purposes only. Certain stock imagery © Thinkstock.

ISBN: 978-1-5127-4866-6 (sc)
ISBN: 978-1-5127-4867-3 (hc)
ISBN: 978-1-5127-4865-9 (e)

Library of Congress Control Number: 2016910858

Print information available on the last page.

WestBow Press rev. date: 07/01/2016

Contents

I dedicate this book to my sweet Thao. His life brought joy unspeakable. He taught me to love unconditionally. He taught me to slow down, to open my eyes, to see beyond the normal everyday of this earthly life. His death brought grief quite unbearable. But he was worth it. And if I could do it again, I would in a heartbeat. And if I had known how his story would go, I would do it anyway. I will forever be changed. I am forever thankful to be Thao's mom.

I also dedicate this book to parents going through hard things. You are not alone.

and if not, He is still good.

—taken from Daniel 3:18

Foreword

Do you believe that Jesus is good and loving? Do you *still* believe, even after great tragedy and unexplainable pain? *Still* is a mother's personal witness of the goodness and the love of the Great Savior in one of the most powerful, painful, broken, and victorious stories I have ever personally experienced. The story of the life and death of Thao Nardoni is about Jesus. It is about Jesus loving and leading His people through real life—Jesus in the real world, where tragedy plays no favorites and where prayers are not always answered in a way that makes any sense to our human minds. Tiffany has created a beautiful reflection of Jesus's presence and faithfulness in the darkest, hardest parts of life. Death is real. Jesus is too.

Life with Jesus is often portrayed as being easy and comfortable. So when tragedy strikes, when a young child dies, people are sent scrambling for answers, real-life answers that can stand up to the storms of life. Is God present in those moments? Is He *still* good? Does He *still* love?

Will Jesus really walk us through the valley of the shadow of death? Is there hope on the other side? Tiffany shares the story of a family's experience with Jesus in the valley of the shadow of death. *Still* is an honest reflection on Jesus in the midst of the storm. Jesus who doesn't freak out when we are confused or angry or stuck in our doubts. Jesus who doesn't make promises that He doesn't plan to keep. Jesus who loves always and is always good. Jesus who is not conformed to our will, but instead is conforming us to His. Jesus who promised two powerful things: "I will be with you always;" and, "I have gone to prepare a place for you." His invitation is pretty simple: "Come follow me."

What does that look like? What happens in the hardest parts of life? Can we follow Jesus when life makes no sense, when prayers aren't answered our way, when the unthinkable becomes our reality? The pages that follow share a powerful story of Jesus in the midst of tragedy and darkness. As you read, you will find a beautiful expression of the faithfulness of God to carry his people through the difficulties of life with sufficient grace and peace. There is no more powerful display of Jesus's shepherding than to watch him walk some of his children through the hardest part of their lives. So as you read, be *still* and know that He is (*still*) God!

—Kurt Sovine, pastor

Introduction

I never pictured myself as a writer. All I ever wanted was to be a wife and mother. God's story in my life is different, though. I've realized over time that my desires, although good, may not be what bring the most glory to Him. I don't really like being center stage; I'd prefer to quietly rock babies in the background. Maybe, just maybe, it's not about me or my comfort. But somewhere along the way, God placed a desire in my heart, a passion to share. It's not really my story anyway; it's God's story, what He has done in my life with my family. I have learned to grow in dependence on Him. And even though this story is born of loss, it is beautiful. Because in the end, all things will be made new. All things will make sense again. I truly believe that I have the choice to sit quietly or to make known what God has done for me in these most difficult times. *Still* is my memoir of my sweet son. *Still* is what I've come to know.

As in, he is *still* my son. Forever and always, a sweet part of my life.

As in, God is *still* good. Forever and always and into eternity. I am not alone.

Even when earthly things fade away.

None of this would be possible without the amazing support of my favorite person, my husband. Jeff, I love you more each day. I am thankful for the life we have shared together. I pray we have many more adventures to come. I am ready to risk it all and live life to the fullest, going and doing whatever God asks of us. Your commitment and love to God is the most wonderful example for me and our children. Thank you for everything you do for our family.

I am also so thankful to many supportive friends. Friends that have listened to me cry, prayed with me and for me, encouraged me when I doubted, given their time and energy, and just all around put up with me during this chaotic time of life. I don't really know what to say, except, thank you for being there. Thank you for being willing to sacrifice so much to help me and my family.

And thank you to my extended family: siblings, grandparents, parents, cousins—you guys rock. You have helped keep memories alive. You have sorted through and dedicated time and energy to this project as if it were your own. A very deep thank you to you all.

I pray that you read this with an open heart. I pray that as I bare my soul, the words reach yours and that you can see even just a glimpse of true hope in Christ Jesus.

—Tiffany

Prologue

I wish I could talk to all the parents of PICU babies.

I have been there.

I have been on the edge of despair. I've clung to the finger twitches, the batting eyes. I've sat on my chair, collapsed on my bed, and paced for what seemed like hours.

I know this place. It's scary and lonely and intense. It's quiet and busy. You get used to the rhythm of the machines, the chatter of the nurses. You get numb to the exhaustion. Hunger almost never strikes. It may even feel hopeless. Or possibly normal.

Passing through the doors of the PICU, you enter into an entirely different world. The outside almost ceases to exist.

It's a world of tests and results. Of decisions and prayer. Of rest and trauma. Of life. And of death.

And yet, life is bustling all around you. The nurses go home to their families, ball games, graduations, and vacations.

Friends visit. Family tries to feed you.

They all beg with their eyes for ways to help.

But you know they know there is nothing they can really do. Because nothing else matters.

So we pray. But we don't pray out of desperation. We pray out of expectation. God answers these prayers.

He answers every single one. He answered all my prayers for my Thao. He sustained Thao's life. God created Thao's life. He gave me my son for five precious years, memories of good times (and hard times), pictures of his smile, videos of his laugh and little voice.

I can't tell you how to feel. I can't tell you it's all going to be okay here on earth. I don't know how your journey with your child will go. But I know who holds the future. I know there is hope. I've been where you are, and I have survived.

All day, every day, I have to choose to trust in the Lord for my children and my life. I have to place my hope in things greater than this earth. Both you and I know that the earthly things don't matter so much anymore.

I don't know how God will answer your prayers. I don't know how or why He sustains life. I know that seeing other children walk out of the hospital is almost more than I can handle sometimes. I know that reading about miracles will many times strike a nerve I didn't know I even had. I know that praying for healing is sometimes a very difficult task for me.

I've been down the road of guilt. I wondered if maybe I didn't have enough faith. I asked God: If I would have thrown my body on Thao, covered him more deeply in faith-filled prayer, would that have worked? Maybe I gave up. What if I would have prayed after he died? What about all these stories of people being clinically dead and coming back to life? What if I would have trusted God more than the machines? What if I would have trusted God instead of medicine?

I've wrestled, you guys. Really crying out to God. Asking Him why I am not good enough. Why didn't He reveal to me what I was supposed to do? Why didn't He give me the faith I needed?

I haven't asked why very much, but when I have, it's been deep and hard and soul-wrenchingly painful. And honestly, I didn't ask why until the newness of his death wore off.

When reality hits so many times, you eventually break. You are weak. But, in that weakness, He is strong.

And in my weakness, He reminded me how strong I am because of Him. Not because of anything I've done or not done. Not because I didn't pray at the right time or the right way.

And I am reminded that He answered every prayer. I'm reminded that we are a part of a bigger plan than I could ever imagine. I'm reminded that God is good. He is faithful.

And His grace covers my doubts in myself.

When I begged God to show me my lack of faith, I was reminded that I desperately knew with my whole being that God could have healed Thao.

And when we took the machines off and Thao breathed sparingly on his own, I remember believing God could make his lungs work. I remember, when I held him and the machines were not doing the job of his organs any longer, that my thought was, *Now God will do His thing.*

I remember begging God to make him breathe.

He didn't.

He answered my prayer, but he didn't make Thao breathe again.

I had begged God to let the suffering end.

And now, three and a half years later, I'm begging God to let me in again. Not necessarily to the suffering, but to that place.

The place of brokenness.

The place of weariness.

The place of believing deep down in my soul, in the sovereignty of God Almighty.

The place of knowing God Himself is the only thing holding me up.

How can I crave such things? How can I long to be in a place that is so painful?

That's where we find God. That's where we find His presence, His mercy, His compassion, His everything. Because that is where we are filled. Because that is where He can lift us up and bring us back to healing.

The healing doesn't always come in ways we expect. The brokenness doesn't always have to be tragic. The weariness doesn't always have to be from loss.

If you haven't been in the place of fighting for your child's next breath, I cannot explain to you the temptation of utter despair or the gentle peace that sweeps over and encompasses the room.

And that's okay, if you don't understand this kind of tragedy.

We can all come to Him broken and weary now. We all fall short. We all need that grace and love and mercy to bring us back to Him.

This place. I want to dwell here.

Friday, June 21, 2013
it is *still* well with my soul

Somewhere, today, there are parents holding their child, just begging him to breathe. There are parents saying good-bye to a child, once so full of life, so full of fight, but now limp in their arms. Parents, once so full of joy at the sight of their newborn child, awed at the miracle of birth, now clinging to the hope of heaven, the promise of fullness, wellness, and eternity with the Creator. And then, here I am, scrubbing floors, fixing lunch, struggling with getting everything done. I go about my business, my new normal, my routine, but not without thinking of these moments I once was a part of. Moments that shaped me, challenged me, hurt me deeper than I thought possible. Moments seeping with unspeakable peace. Moments I oddly long for at times, just to be nearer that time when I could feel his hand gently squeeze mine. In those moments, I didn't think of anything else. The days that followed were just ... there.

I imagine outsiders looking in, seeing the worst being over—the shock, the loss, the funeral. The most difficult are the days to follow, the days when the new normal, forever-ness becomes reality. Nothing really matters so much anymore. Things are just things. The temptation to hold tighter to my children while I still can emerges, but I fight back. I do life again, so many times forcing normalcy for whatever reason. I fight the guilt and sorrow from shattered dreams of Ava having her best friend, her big brother, stand up for her in high school; of Thao and Liam playing baseball together in the backyard; of Thao begging me to ride somewhere, anywhere with a freshly licensed sixteen-year-old Uncle Trey. I don't hold my children or my husband or my own life so tightly. I have learned that my meager attempts at control are just that—attempts.

For so much of my life, I tried to reason, fix, plan, and figure it all out. Who am I trying to fool? I never could get Thao to take his medicine or eat meat, I failed at convincing Ava she really doesn't know how to play piano without lessons, and Liam totally has me wrapped around his finger at naptime. ("Awwwwww, Mama ... awwww." All while rubbing my face and kissing me.) I'm reminded once again that I want to be at that place again. That place where peace and comfort from Christ are surrounding my moments. When I am slightly annoyed at my so-called failures, I remember what is really important. It's not the half-completed landscaping or the unmade beds or even the bag of chip crumbs that spilled *all over the house.* (Okay, that matters a little.)

No, it's seeing Christ and his blessings in every moment. Seeing the strong will as a gift, for we had a fighter! Seeing the pureness of her heart and free spirit as creativity and innocence. Seeing the extra snuggles instead of the extra time it takes to get him to sleep. My prayer is to be so sensitive to these moments that I don't forget the power of the peace of Christ. I want to live the rest of my life holding loosely the material things of this world, and dearly close to my heart what truly matters.

Each chapter of this book is precious to me. As I read back through, I realize my thoughts may seem scattered to you. I realize there is a lot of reflection, many memories, and probably errors. Each chapter, though, reminds me of a gift. A moment or time that God gave me. I agonized over the titles, because what perfectly reflects the goodness of God? I hope you can see the goodness of the Lord throughout—because He truly is our good Father.

CHAPTER 1

Reflection

Sometimes, I just close my eyes and picture him. I remember his smile. His soft voice. His gentle touch with his baby brother. I remember how he and his sister, Ava, were such good friends (most of the time). Sometimes, I even forget how much I miss him. Not because it goes away, but because I don't always let myself go there. It has been three years. It's not fresh, but it's not gone. There are days when that part of my life really seems more like a different life rather than a few years ago.

And all I can think right now is how much I want to hug him. I have no words. Sometimes no feelings, even.

I mean, really, I cannot begin to describe to you the range of emotions. I don't even know. Anything. Everything. Nothing. There's deep sorrow. And hope. There are so many words. And then there are none.

There are moments like now, right now, when I keep thinking I just need to power through. I need to just wake up each day and keep going. I need to write. I need to finish what I've started. I need to do what God has asked of me.

1

So I beg Him to give me the words. The memories. The stories. Help me, Lord, to remember my son.

But when the memories come pouring in, it's like a floodgate has opened, and all I can do is want to hold him. Just to wrap my arms around and hold him close, just once more. To feel him sink into me, like my other children do. To kneel down and embrace the hug. To brush his wispy hair away from his eyes.

There just are no words to describe the sense of longing, the pain of loss, and the feeling of grief. I cannot breathe. I let the tears come, and finally, I relent. Because as much as the pain overwhelms my soul, I want to remember him.

With all of my being, I want the sting of loss to be near because then—and only then—will the impact of his life, the reality of him, and the wholeness of my son always be with me. He was the start of my day. Now his name rests at the tip of my tongue.

Many people look at me and think because my son died my life is forever changed. I want to tell you that because my son was conceived, my life is forever changed. That is where his story began. That is where my love for him started. That is when I became Thao's mom. And that is when the fears and worries came. It's also when God started working on me to give it all up to Him. That is when I had to begin trusting the Lord with my son, my most precious treasure. My everything.

Sunday, August 3, 2014
Changed

It's hard to admit sometimes, but I guess I've changed since Thao died. But then again, I changed when Thao was born.

Sometimes, it's difficult to think about his sickness, symptoms, and death. The what-ifs. The what-only. The why. The blame game. The guilt. The silence.

I sometimes get angry with myself. I tell myself I should have done more, prayed more, and been a better mom. I should have spent less time researching and trying to figure him out and just *be*.

That's not the mom I was. And that's not even the mom I am now. I hate the fact that I've changed sometimes. I'm older. I've experienced more with my children. I've learned. That's really important—I've learned some things. I've acquired knowledge that I wasn't just born with.

Because who knows what to do to make your child better all the time? Or listen all the time? And then there's that little thing about the past. And reacting. And regrets. Oh. My. Goodness. Parenting is *so* hard.

For much of Thao's short life, I begged God for answers and for miracles. Just something.

I so badly wanted Him to reveal to me what I was supposed to do.

I just wanted one little miracle. I just wanted my son to be healthy. I wanted him to be healthy so he wouldn't hurt, so he wouldn't feel left out, so he'd have lots of friends—and so I'd be a better mom. I wanted him to be healthy so I wouldn't have to spend so much time trying so hard.

I wanted it to be easy. It was easy to love him. It was easy to fight for him. It just wasn't enough. I loved him with my entire being. And I still missed it.

He was my miracle.

I always knew he was a gift from God, the precious child I had prayed for. Curly hair and blue eyes, with a slight grin that would make any person's heart melt.

He was worth every tear past and every tear yet to come. I'd fight for him all over again. Those were some of the hardest, best, and most treasured years. And I thank the Lord for the miracle of his little life, his strong personality, and the ability to remember.

I have changed.

Thao's life changed me. He sent me, on my knees, to our Lord. He gave me beautiful memories. He inspired me to be more passionate, loving, and adventurous. He made me worry and taught me to relax. He *is* my gift from God. And I am so thankful to have been changed by him.

There are things in this world that I will never understand. Things that happen this side of heaven don't often make sense to us.

This side of heaven ...

Those words truly resonate with me now.

I lost my son. My firstborn child. The child who made me a mother. He made dreams come true. He made strangers smile with those sparkling blue eyes. He made the PICU (pediatric intensive care unit) nurses fall in love with him without saying a word.

He was an old soul. He was a gift. He was my sweet Thao.

I cannot put into words the depth of this child. I want to share with you the person who changed my life more drastically than anyone else. I wish I could share this part of my heart to the very depth of the hole that was left when he died, but there is no way.

I read obituaries so differently now. How can you truly sum up one person's entire existence into a few short paragraphs? How do I describe to you what we are missing now?

The dash. I've heard it before; I've seen the grave markers.

Jeffrey Thao Nardoni

August 25, 2006–January 13, 2012

But the dash. So much filled that short little dash. His was only five years, yet so full. So many words I wanted to say. Many people were touched by Thao's life, and for that, I am so thankful.

And that didn't end when the little dash did. Thao's life continues to touch others. Why God chose me to be the mother of such a special gift, I will never know—this side of heaven.

Sunday, February 23, 2014
Dear Thao

If I could write a letter ...

Dear Thao,

Not until now did I feel the need to write down these memories and feelings as though I could actually write a letter to you. Maybe it's because life is getting busier and full again. Maybe it's because I feel so far away from you and the phase of my life that you were physically a part of. Maybe it's because I don't always look around for you like I once did. That hurts. A lot.

Oh, my dear, sweet Thao. I don't miss you any less than I did the day you left us. Truth be told, I missed you before that. I missed you every time I left you. I missed you when you went to sleep. There were days I wanted to wake you so I could hold you longer. There were days I would snuggle with you or kiss your face after you were asleep. I secretly (or not so secretly) loved it when you would crawl into bed with us. I'm sorry I wasn't more of a morning person. Maybe I should have let you stay up later than I did. (Okay, not really.)

I can still hear your voice, your jokes, and your questions. I miss the conversations. Recently, I've wondered what our conversations would consist of if you were here. You'd be seven and a half years old now. I cannot even imagine. Yet, I can. I can imagine you chasing Liam around the house with Nerf guns, building forts, and tormenting Ava. I can imagine you and Ava playing games while Liam naps. I can imagine that you would be more patient than I am while teaching Ava how to read or teaching Liam his shapes and colors. I can only imagine what crazy creations you'd be making in the kitchen. I sometimes bake late at night, because the others don't enjoy it like you did. I imagine I would have let you stay up late on those nights. I loved my alone time with you. I don't often bake anymore. It's just not the same without you.

Sometimes I listen to Daddy working in the basement and I think about how quiet it must be for him. You were such a good helper to both of us. It hurts to think about the dried-up Play-Doh and rusted cookie cutters. You were always by our sides, helping or creating, spending time with us.

So much has changed. There are things that we cannot prepare ourselves for, and there are things we thought we had. Truly, there is no way to prepare for life without you. Right now, you seem so far away. I promised you we'd be there soon, and we will, but from this side, it feels like forever.

Ava told me today she wishes that there were no heaven so that no one would die. She misses you like crazy. If she only knew, if we all only knew, how wonderful heaven is, maybe we'd be more content to miss you.

I often feel cheated. I feel like you and I (and the rest of our family) are missing out on so much. You told me you were going to live with me forever. And you did. And sometimes I think about how often I cried and prayed over you. I think about all the pain, but mostly I think about how overwhelmingly blessed I am to be your mom. Your peaceful spirit and strong will, your love for life, your passion, taught me so much about myself and about God in all his mercy. The pain is worth it, my son. Each day that goes by, we are one day closer to being in Glory with you, held by Jesus himself and no longer living with the hole of missing you. It's worth every tear, Thao. Every painful conversation. I'd do it over a million times. And we will.

We are so thankful for the five beautiful years we had with you.

Soon.

I love you, my Thao.

CHAPTER 2

Change

Thao had been sick for a while. Honestly, he was sick off and on for a long time. Years. And since he was only five, that really meant he was sick for his entire life. This time was different. For a while, we thought he was doing better. Jeff and I had been searching for so long. We desperately wanted to help him, as all parents of sick children do. We cried out to God. We struggled. We wanted answers and healing. We wanted control of this situation that seemed to be controlling us. Yet, we had no idea what the enemy was.

Thao was a sweet, snuggly baby. Normal development, no signs of anything except pure amazing-ness. (Yes, I know. As you continue to read, you will notice that I am madly in love with my family—please, keep reading.)

I am the mom who reads all the possible side effects for medications, because it was very common for Thao to have a reaction. His immune system, no matter how hard we tried to boost it, just didn't seem to keep up with him.

But thankfully, my strong-willed son did not let that stop him much. Until it did.

It stopped us all. It was right before Christmas, December 8, 2011. Thao, Ava, Liam, and I were heading to visit my sister. Thao had been sick for a while. It started with bronchitis, but the medication he was given seemed to make him worse. It had been three days. I wanted to seize the day. Make memories. I wanted something joyful in the midst of the sickness. I also wanted Thao to eat—anything. So I pulled into McDonald's and let them get *whatever they wanted*. Let me tell you, this was a *big* deal. I was/am a strict, "fast food and sugar in small quantities; here's a list of what my children are allowed to eat" mom. I know this, my willingness to let go of that and let my little ones make memories, was yet another gift from God.

Thao got an M&M McFlurry. But not before asking me if I was serious—and giving me a look that said he thought I had lost it. (Although he was fully willing to take advantage of it!)

That night, Jeff came home, and we knew something wasn't right. Thao was usually very quick, very on top of things, intuitive, smart. He couldn't sleep, and since he had napped, we just assumed he was getting better. We brought him downstairs to watch *The Dick Van Dyke Show* with us (one of our favorites).

He was confused. He asked to watch it again. It was already playing. He started seeing things: spots, colors. He was making his "angry face" at me for no reason. He couldn't answer our questions.

We knew something was terribly wrong. We called our good friend and neighbor to come sit with the littler ones. We called my mom to come take over for him. As we were leaving, I remember telling Jeff which hospital to go to. He was surprised at the one I chose, but I know God was leading me. I know God was the voice, the strong, secure, calming spirit that washed over me that night.

Because I thought we were losing him on the way to the hospital. But we didn't.

I praise Jesus for that. Because I know, deep down in my soul, I knew then, he was near meeting Jesus that night.

I remember the freedom of holding Thao, just holding him while we waited for the results of the dreaded lab work. I whispered to him how much I loved him.

The results came in. The words. *Kidney failure. Transfer. Peoria. Children's hospital. Immediately.*

The weather wasn't friendly that night. He would be taken by ambulance, even though they preferred to airlift him.

Dialysis.

My head was spinning, but outside, I was calm. I asked my Thao who loved him. It was a game we always played.

"You, Mommy."

"Yes," I said, choking back tears, wondering if this was the last time I would be able to hold him and say these words. I had to make sure he knew.

It's amazing how many thoughts enter your head in these moments. It's amazing what you remember. How vivid the memories still are. What a gift from God.

"Who else loves you?"

"Daddy."

"And who else?"

"Ava."

"And?"

"Liam."

"And?"

"Jesus."

"Yes." He knew. I knew that he knew. His mind was clear enough to answer these very important questions. This was another gift. Thank you, Lord, for moments of clarity in crisis.

And then I remember asking Jeff a question that I already knew the answer to. I remember looking deep into his eyes and asking him to please stay with Thao, no matter what, to please take care of our son.

I am glad he wasn't upset with me for asking such a silly question. Yes, he would ride with Thao; he wouldn't leave our child's side.

Then I left.

And I looked back, peered around the corner to say my last good-bye. Because I thought it might be the last.

"I love you."

And then Thao winked. He smiled and winked. His beautiful, comforting wink. It was another one of God's gifts to me.

I remember the nurse commenting on it. I remember thinking, *Oh, you don't even know the comfort that the simplest wink from my boy brings. It's still him, through whatever is messing around with his body and mind, I still have him here. Not all is lost.*

I left the hospital. I tried to drive home. I live five minutes from the hospital, but I forgot how to get home. It was a blur, but I made it. I made it inside. And I somehow managed to throw a few clothes together. I grabbed Liam, because he wasn't quite five months old and was still nursing. He needed me.

Liam typically screamed in the car, but I took him anyway. I packed enough for three days. And I left Ava with my mom.

I made decisions in those moments that were very real and quick. I responded to this crisis with peace and sense and stability because somehow, I knew I wasn't alone. I knew that God was

12

leading and guiding every decision, every choice. And I knew that Thao had that same peace. Jesus was close.

On the way to the hospital, which was two hours away, I knew Thao wasn't okay. I had someone tell me my life would be right again. But I knew it would never be the same. At one point, Jeff called me. I thought we had lost Thao. I was prepared to hear the words.

But they didn't come.

I realized I was holding my breath. I breathed again, closed my eyes, and prayed.

"Thank you, Lord, for sustaining Thao's life."

So, we drove, and Liam slept. Jesus was close. I knew this was another gift from God. I know the Lord cares about the small things. Noticing these small gifts from God in these very real crisis moments kept me sane. Little did I know how much peace I would gain from noticing these blessings. I thank the Lord for opening my eyes. This is not a natural instinct for a mom. *I should shut down. I should be done. I should give up.* But I didn't—and I won't.

As I called my closest friends and watched the snow start to fall, I prayed, *"Lord Jesus, please don't take him yet. I **need** him still. I want him. I love him too much."*

> "But now, Lord, what do I look for?
> My hope is in you." (Psalm 39:7)

As we drove in silence, I opened my Bible. I prayed for comfort, and He answered me with this verse. I knew deep in my soul that my life would never be the same. I knew things weren't going to be okay. I knew, but I wouldn't admit it. I had hope. I *have* hope. I wasn't worried or anxious. I tried to wrap my head around my new circumstances, but I was in crisis mode. I wasn't even capable of processing. I couldn't do the what-ifs yet. I was just there—not numb, not crying. I was placing my hope, my Thao, my future, my focus in Him.

This was the beginning of a new journey. Of peace I never knew existed. Of pain I had only feared. Of a new life filled with loss and joy, of faith and grace. Of longing and contentment.

A new life where I suddenly felt out of place in my earthly home. Where my heart was drilled with holes, to be filled with only Jesus. Where I no longer cared about any material possessions.

Yes, my sweet, comfortable, safe life was, from then on, just a beautiful memory.

I was thankful for a safe trip, for family that lives close, dear friends, and church family. I was thankful because by the time I got to the hospital, my sister-in-law was there, waiting to take Liam from me.

I walked down the hall. Across from the nurses' station was a room with glass walls. I didn't realize then, but the most critical patients are assigned these rooms. That's where my Thao was.

I was greeted by a kind doctor. His voice said that Thao had been asking for me. I had a million unanswered questions, but no one knew the answers, and I understood that. So I sat on the bed with my Thao. His fever was high again.

Jeff and I just sat there. Watching. Trying to answer questions. Trying to stay out of the way. Trying to understand. It was a whirlwind. But everyone was calm, steady, and kind.

We needed to get Thao on dialysis. Jeff and I had to leave for part of this procedure, but Thao was sedated. We went out to the waiting room, which was full of familiar faces. It was daylight. I vaguely remember somebody handed me an envelope of money.

I remember people trying to get me to eat and sleep. I wasn't hungry or tired. I didn't even know what time it was, or how long we had been there. It was maybe around 7:00 a.m.

Dialysis started. We went back to see him. We were introduced to so many people. I didn't realize, then, that these people would become my family for the next five weeks—that our lives would be forever changed just by knowing them. I didn't know I would grow to love them, or that they would grow to love my son, who still refused to talk to them.

We learned a few things that day. They began to figure out what was wrong with him, a diagnosis of Hemolytic Uremic Syndrome. HUS is typically caused by a primary infection such as E.coli, leading to the premature breakdown of red blood cells and eventually clogging the kidney and causing kidney failure. I sat with a paper and scribbled letters, trying to make sense of it all. One of our specialists asked us if we understood how sick he was.

We did. I think. It was all just so much.

We had been searching, researching for years to try to find answers. Was this what we had been looking for? They said something about three to four weeks for kidney recovery.

We'd just have to wait. We settled in next to Thao for the wait. We were in this together.

That night, December 9, out of desperation, we booked a hotel room. There must have been ten of us in that small room. Jeff stayed at the hospital with Thao. At this point, I was still nursing Liam, and

I wasn't willing to give that up. I was concerned for his health. We still didn't have concrete answers about the cause of Thao's illness, and germs lurked in the hospital. To me, the safest and most sensible thing was to still nurse Liam, to at least try to keep his immune system strong.

I showered that night. It felt like it had been months. This is when I finally cried. I didn't even know where to begin.

My son's five-year-old body was quitting on him. His kidneys were failing. We were in the pediatric intensive care unit. Our lives were turned upside down. Our boy with eyes that sparkled blue lay in a hospital bed, tied down with tubes.

Earlier that day, we thought he had been on the road to recovery. Sunday, just a few days before, he had been a little sick, so we took him to the emergency room that afternoon. We knew a few people who'd recently had pneumonia, and, contagious or not, we weren't up for chancing it. He seemed to get sick so often, no matter what we did to try to build up his little immune system. He charmed the employees at the hospital even that day. He sat on the bed and laughed at me. I didn't know how to play Angry Birds, but he was showing me. They concluded he had bronchitis, took a chest x-ray to be sure, prescribed antibiotics, let him pick out a handmade stuffed animal, and sent us home.

When I asked him what he was going to name his little dinosaur, he told me, in classic Thao style, he was saving it for Ava's Christmas gift. It was only December 4, but that was my boy—always thinking ahead, so thoughtful. So we went home and hid the sweet gift.

The next morning, Thao still could not keep the antibiotic down. We made an appointment with our family doctor. He ended up with a shot of Rocephin, stronger antibiotics. In the three days that followed, Thao had stopped eating. This was not our boy. No matter how sick our child got, he was *always, always, always* thinking about food—planning the next meal or snack, what we were going to bake, or trying to figure out what Jeff and I had eaten after he went to bed the night before. His breakfasts usually consisted of several courses. I'm serious when I say I was terrified when he lost his appetite.

After three days and many phone calls with our doctor, he seemed to improve. He was laughing and trying to eat. That day didn't end as I'd thought it would. I was hoping for rest, but instead, we spent the night traveling to the children's hospital.

There I was, in the hotel. I was alone. The hot water felt so good, but it wasn't washing away the terrible dream that had become my reality. I had left half my family in the hospital. I cried for a long time in the shower. I cried out to God. I cried for Thao. My little sidekick.

CHAPTER 3

Strong Will

In April 2011, I was pregnant for the sixth time. At twenty-seven years old, I had been married seven years to my favorite person ever, had two perfectly beautiful children, and a new baby on the way. Spring was a breath of fresh air for me. Spring represented this new season in my life—beauty of warmth and light, after a cold, dark winter.

Jeff and I had experienced loss. Three of my precious babies were lost through miscarriage before we could hold them. My heart ached for more children, but I had a renewed sense of gratitude for the ones I did have. I was maturing in my faith as I learned to give things to our Lord. As I let go of more, I also grew to be a more confident mother. I embraced motherhood from day one. It was my dream come true.

Except it wasn't.

It wasn't my dream to have three pregnancies end that way. It wasn't my dream to have a difficult time dealing with the loss, or to then struggle for answers to questions I didn't even know I had. It most definitely was not my dream for Thao to be sick. Invisibly sick.

But I was learning to let go of control, to open windows and let the sunlight in. That spring, I learned that naps were not as important as I'd once thought. I learned that sometimes, you have to look for puddles to jump in. I learned to listen more and speak less. I learned a lot about grace. God's grace for me, who tried so hard to find answers, figure it all out, and plan, plan, plan ...

And as I listened and learned more, I did become a more confident mom. I was confident because I was learning how incapable I am. I didn't know the answers, and I wasn't ever going to figure it all out, but I was beginning to see a God that just wanted me to come to Him.

Grace is fascinating to me. I began to see it all around me. Examples of God's grace were just begging to be found by my hungry eyes. I will never forget a particularly hard day with Thao. He was four years old and the most strong-willed child I had ever known. At times, I was convinced he hated me. Looking back, I realize I should not have let a four-year-old's angry words cut to my heart as much as I did. But I also could never, ever imagine saying such hurtful words.

He was sent to time out for one reason or another (most of the time, it was because our child was *obsessed* with sweet treats, and he would sneak them). Some days, Thao would comply to his four minutes of sitting in the hallway, but this was not that day. Thao screamed at me for what felt like hours. He yelled mean things like, "I don't like you!" or "I want Daddy!" or "I am so mad at you!"

Okay, it sounds so silly now, but seriously, I promise, he meant it in the moment. And it hurt me. This child was making me a stronger person.

And then, after the screaming, spitting, and head-butting on the wall was over, he did this crazy thing. He stopped. He said he was done. He came over to me, apologized with a hug, and then ... asked me to bake cookies with him.

I did not feel like baking cookies with him. My chest was hurting, my head pounding. My son had just rejected me in four-year-old style. I had yelled back, complete with tears and hurtful words.

And yet, he wanted me. He knew I always loved him. He forgave me for those hurtful words I'd spoken to him, and he wanted to spend time with me again.

Grace.

I finally understood. Grace is the beautiful existence of love, sacrifice, forgiveness, and some kind of steadfastness that I cannot comprehend.

As I learned about grace, I also started counting my blessings. I did this for myself at first. I longed for contentment and joy. Freedom from envy and guilt. So I began seeing more things than just my husband and children as blessings. I didn't want to take them for granted any longer. I was finished being the distracted, worried mom who couldn't let go of all the bad stuff. I wanted to be fully present, loving the moments, and I wanted my kids to remember me as a parent full of God's grace.

I began to seek God more. Although parenting with Jeff was my dream life, I knew I would fail miserably without God. The Lord was working in my heart to be still. There was joy in the quiet, in the stillness. There was joy in giving up the worries of having a perfectly clean house. That spring and summer, we cherished our moments, we talked about Jesus. We played. We skipped a lot of naps. I was able to relax and enjoy my family in a way I hadn't before. In a way that wasn't laden with guilt of a to-do list.

Little did I know what God was preparing my heart for and how thankful I would be for these little lessons later on.

April 28, 2011
Thank the Lord

Thank the Lord for every kick, wiggle, squirm, (backache, craving, and swollen foot). I just read a mother's blog about delivering her baby twenty weeks early. I've experienced loss with miscarriage, but I've never held my twenty-week-old baby, who never caught a breath, and laid her in a coffin. I've never had to explain to my children about the death of a sibling, although I've thought about the situation before. I've grieved for my three babies, but I know they are with Jesus. I'm so thankful for the comfort and rest we have in that. Today, I will take time to be thankful for all the little things that maybe yesterday I missed.

1. The way the sun is shining in my living room, gently showing off the dust that needs attention but reminding me it can wait.
2. The echo of children's feet on the hardwood floors, oblivious to time, and still in their jammies.

3. A beautiful, sunshiny day following a day of exhaustion, rain, and a leaky basement.

4. An almost empty laundry basket (because what else do you do when you are too tired to function in normal capacity?).

5. The remnants of a fort that turned into a train, house, and restaurant, and was used to make fun memories on a gloomy day.

6. Remembering my four-year-old's two things he was thankful for at bedtime the other day: Daddy coming home for lunch, and all the special things we got to do (eating ice cream out).

7. My two-year-old sliding down the stairs this morning, full of smiles, crazy hair, and sporting her upside-down sunglasses, in her princess jammies.

8. My sweet, patient husband never complaining about dealing with my meltdowns of emotional insanity (enough said).

9. The thought of my son carrying around a new treasure (which happens to be an old corduroy vest he found while cleaning out my grandpa's garage).

10. Every time we play pretend, the good guy wins, and the bad guy really is a little good anyway.

There were many ups and downs in those days that followed in the hospital. There were times I would look with sad eyes on the people whose children weren't getting any better. I was worried that I would appear too excited and happy when Thao was getting better. On good days, I felt as thought I was bouncing through the halls of that now familiar place. God answered so many prayers. Prayers that we didn't even know needed to be said. We spent a few nights in the family housing, but it was smaller than a hotel room, and not very accommodating for a three-year-old and a five-month-old to spend their days. Neither was the hospital waiting room, but those were our only options.

God answered our prayers for a better temporary home for our children. He answered bigger and better than we expected. We were set to rent a house; God provided a three-bedroom apartment, fully furnished and five minutes from the hospital.

At this point, we were making arrangements to move there indefinitely. Jeff was staying at the hospital overnight, and I was in our new home with the little two—and so many others. Family came. Friends came. Strangers donated. Neighbors took care of our home in Danville. We were given meals, gift cards. God provided everything we needed and more. Our dear friends literally moved in with us while we were in Peoria. God had provided them with a job that allowed them to drop everything and come from twelve hours away—indefinitely. God is good. We were so blessed.

But the roller coaster of Thao's health continued. He never was a textbook child. I would joke about it all the time. I taught preschool, studied early childhood—but Thao was unique. He was the most strong-willed child I had ever known. And I wasn't the only one who thought that.

One particular night in the hospital, Thao refused to take his Tylenol (which was completely normal for him). This sweet nurse was so good with him. She was the only one Thao spoke to.

"I am so mad at you!" he said to her.

And she only smiled. She and I worked tirelessly to get him to take it. After quite the battle and several bribes, we succeeded ...

Only we hadn't. Thao fell asleep, and about an hour later, Tylenol started dripping out of his mouth.

Yes, that was Thao. He never ceased to amaze me. Doctors had struggled to figure out what was physically wrong with him. Yet, they were always in awe of his comprehension, his conversations.

I would like to say he was brilliant. (Here I go again!) But he truly loved learning. He was also self-conscious. We couldn't praise him too much or he'd stop what he was doing. He embarrassed easily. But our conversations were deep and meaningful. He only spoke when there was something to say. And he didn't start to speak until he had grown confident in that. Even at two and a half years old, he was barely speaking to anyone. We weren't worried. He had mastered his own little sign language. We had started teaching him some signs but stopped, thinking it was delaying his speech. No worries, he just created his own!

After a doctor's appointment when he was two, he signed that he wanted another monkey sticker, please. And then that he wanted to go to Steak 'n Shake for a milkshake.

When the doctor saw our conversation, she was amazed. He was stubborn, but he knew what he wanted, and he didn't rest until he had made it clear. He was a master at negotiating.

February 22, 2010

Jeff and Thao are making applesauce cake with chocolate chips. That was the compromise.

March 25, 2010

Thao at bedtime tonight: "How about I can have eleven donuts after my night-night?"

Me: "No, how about one *and* something healthy?"

Thao: "Okay two."

Jeff: "He's so good at that!"

It's hard not to laugh!

December 24, 2011
My Sweet Thao

How to balance it all? I know many of you already know where we are right now. No one ever imagines that they'd be spending Christmas in the hospital. I have so much to say; yet, the strength to put all my thoughts into words is just not there right now. If you have Facebook, search for "Thao Nardoni Updates," a group we have created to share what is going on with my sweet five-year-old, Thao. I've said often in my blog, he's stubborn, strong-willed, and very adventurous. I'm now convinced that God gave him that extra bit of will for this reason. He's a fighter; that's for sure!

This Christmas Eve morning, I've been reading *Narnia* to my quiet boy, over the sound of machines doing everything that his body can't right now. I have been trying to remember what normal is like. My favorite memory at this moment: "Mom, can you play my favorite song?" Then watching him climb up into his favorite chair and sit and sing, "Here I Am to Worship" while Ava danced and sang along.

I keep telling myself I'm going to write down all these thoughts, these memories, but I just haven't been able to. I pray that I can remember.

If I just have one more day to bring my baby home, he will get donuts for breakfast. He will get to paint the living room his skin color so he's camouflaged. He will get to pick out a kitten. I may even let him play out in the snow. We'll bake, whatever creations he concocts. We'll experiment. We'll build forts. Maybe we'll just bring the snow inside. He can jump on the couch if he wants.

God is giving us incredible peace, but He never said it would be easy. Thao knows Jesus's love, his peace, and feels His strong arms around him, probably more than any of us could even imagine. I keep waking up with the song "I Surrender All" going through my head. I love my Thao, but God loves him more.

Thank you for your prayers. We need them as we desperately try to balance normalcy for Ava and Liam and strength for Thao.

CHAPTER 4

A Storm

Tuesday, June 7, 2011

I love watching them grow and learn. And I know everyone says to enjoy it because it goes so fast. I am enjoying it, but it's still going too fast. I want to treasure the innocent, worry-free attitude that Ava has. Praying that she keeps her joy in Christ, even when she realizes not everything is pink and sparkly. I want to calm Thao's fears, pointing him to Christ for the answers to his undeniably real, fearful questions. I want to protect my children without hovering. I want to discipline them in love without getting angry. I want them to know I love them and cherish the moments I have with them. I have good reasons to write, don't I? But I have even better reasons (some days) not to!

Our little Liam was born the summer of 2011 in the midst of God showing me to enjoy the moments. *Moments.* Just that word brings flashes of smiles, laughter, swimming, and bike rides. I can almost hear the crunching of leaves under my feet as I led my older two children on walks in the woods that fall. I can feel the breeze as I rock a newborn on the porch swing, listening to a brother and sister discuss cicadas and leaves and dinosaurs.

They say hindsight is 20/20. I actually think it's sometimes how God reveals himself. There are moments in my life that I can look back and see God's hand gently leading me. The whispers of His grace motivating me to make decisions in life that now I look back with thankfulness and awe.

And as summer was drawing to a close, new phases of life were beginning to show themselves. It was in those phases that I remember some of the most grace-filled moments of Thao's life. He was becoming a little man, always an old soul, complete with soul-searching conversations. He challenged me in ways I never thought possible. He was strong-willed, passionate, adventurous and absolutely loving life.

I feel like I tell the same stories over and over. Let's face it; that's all I have. If you are reading this, you probably already know that fall was the last season we spent with Thao. And really, that's what this book is about, a memoir about his life. A retrospective view, with flashes of stories about my son's sweet life.

I was alone in my car about three weeks before, driving through the country—corn fields, fluffy white clouds, and blue skies that reach the heavens. I flashed back to that day in the car when I had this "storm" conversation with Thao. It was a very similar fall day, crisp and beautiful. Thao and I were having one of those deep, heart-to-heart conversations, one in which he had been quietly contemplating and finally had the chance to ask the questions. He was in awe of the weather, constantly checking the radar, preparing for storms, making paper boats, and even collecting hail with Jeff and keeping it in the freezer. We made snow ice cream and learned about the different kinds of clouds. He loved it. That particular day he had some good questions, like: "I really wonder why God made the really bad tornadoes. I know why he made the little storms. But I really wonder why he made the bad ones."

Oh, my sweet, contemplative boy. Why did God make the big storms? Little storms are fun. But why the big ones that hurt people, that leave people without shelter and food?

"Well, Thao, I don't know for sure, but maybe it's because we can learn more about how big God is. Maybe it's so we can rely on Him more. We can depend on Him more. He can get us through."

We need Him. He doesn't send the bad storms, but He does get us through them. I was learning to rely on God more. To give to Him my most treasured, my children. To turn over every worry and fear I had about parenting. Once again, I look back on this and see God's hand in the moments, guiding me, teaching me, preparing me for the really big storm I was about to face.

"I will say to the LORD, 'My refuge and my fortress,
my God, in whom I trust.'" (Psalm 92:1)

Three years later, as this conversation played over in my head, I began to pray. To ask God again, what am I supposed to learn from these storms? It was like He whispered to me as I cried to Him, "I am faithful. Forever. I am your Refuge. My plan is certain and perfect and you will not understand. Trust me. And treasure the moments you have."

Saturday, September 3, 2011
This and That: The Things You Forget to Remember

This crazy thought *literally* crossed my mind: *What if something tragic happens tonight and my kids don't know how simply crazy I am about how cute they are?* Okay, here's the dramatic side of me coming out, I know. Seriously, I've been "writing" blogs out in my mind every day. This one in particular I've written, rewritten, and added to probably a dozen times already. (I've actually thought about how nice it would be to be able just to think my blogs and somehow have them written through my thoughts—too much *Meet the Robinsons*, perhaps?) Anyway, here is a list of cute little things that I'm sure to forget someday. I wake up every morning to children who are getting older, doing new and bigger-kid things. Inevitably, they will become adults.

The sweet little things Ava says:

"Hold you me;" "noisy home" (nursing home); "booshie" (smoothie); "roashie" (roast beef);

"bank-bank" (her blankie, okay, that will always
be bank-bank)

Liam's noises: the soft, loud, hungry, irritated,
sleepy cries, whimpers, grunting, "you're gonna
pick me up" noise; "food, what a relief" noise

Thao's incredible ideas for inventions and
recipes. His utter amazement with the weather. And
the questions, oh, the questions. "I really wonder
why God made the really bad tornadoes. I know why
He made the little storms. But I really wonder why
He made the bad ones."

I love my kids. I am beginning to think every
age is my favorite.

Christmastime is a magical time. Full of hope and happiness.
Surrounded by family, gifts, and good food. Thao was my skeptic. I
don't even know why, but he naturally questioned almost everything.
Some things just made sense, but others, like how Santa Claus could
possibly carry toys all over the world to all the children or fit through
a chimney—honestly, I'm not sure what his doubts were exactly,
because he never expressed them. He just gave us the "look." This
classic Thao look meant he was skeptical of the words coming from
your mouth. It was often followed by, "If you say so!"

And that was how his Christmas was when he was four years
old and Ava was two. Everything was magical to her. She hung on
to every word her big Bubba said. Thankfully, Thao was mature
enough, even at four, not to share his doubts with her. He went

along with all the Christmasy traditions. We focus more on Jesus, His birth, His sacrifice, His presence, but Santa is a game we play. I know there are a lot of people that don't do Santa, but we do. It's fun. It's a game. It's a part of the magical Christmas that I enjoy, because at some point, kids grow up and real life hits. Sometimes, it hits hard.

The Christmas that Thao was four, we made his favorite chocolate chip muffins for Christmas morning. We wrapped gifts. We praised Jesus for coming to Earth. We sang songs. We made our traditional peanut butter-ball candy. We decorated a gingerbread house. Thao was a shepherd in his first Christmas play. We wrote a note to Santa on Christmas Eve. We put out cookies and milk and carrots for the reindeer.

I will never forget the look on Thao's face that Christmas morning when Santa had eaten the cookies and had written back to him. As he peered over his muffin, his eyes sparkled. It was a look that said, "This guy might be legit." It was a child's look of wonder. It was magical.

Only one year later, this was our first Christmas with all three kids. I had literally been dreaming of this day for several weeks. It was supposed to be another magical, quiet Christmas at home. Beautiful chaos. Paper strewn all over. Sweet treats. Gifts. Fully enjoying the moments. Playing together. Remembering baby Jesus and the true gift we have been given.

My dream of a perfect Christmas was shattered. We were in the hospital, reading *Narnia*, watching the stillness, listening to the machines, sitting next to Thao as he was fighting for his life. I fought Christmas. I fought it hard.

I told everyone we would celebrate when Thao came home. I didn't care where or when, but our Christmas would wait until he woke up. Thao hadn't been awake since December 21. He was intubated, medicated. He was fighting hard, but his body was fighting against him. We were still struggling to understand what we were up against.

There was a peace that filled that room that I cannot even explain. A peace that passes understanding. Nurses fell in love with my still, small boy. Doctors gave up vacations with family to stay close to him. Doctors offered us their homes to live in. Friends gave up their Christmas plans. People drove for hours to visit, to stay with our other children. We were so blessed. We were surrounded by people that showed us truly what it meant to love each other as Christ loves us. Everyone gave their all, crying out in prayer.

In these moments of despair and frustration, we often begin to wonder what God wants from us. So we offer Him things, we bargain, we beg, we plead. We may even threaten. But you see, the thing is, I fasted in prayer for my boy; I cried out to Him. I didn't filter my feelings to God. And God didn't freak out. The difference between me and God is that God is sovereign. He has the whole picture laid out in front of Him, and I can only see a few inches in front of my face. So I can beg and bargain with God, but ultimately, He just wants *me*. He wants my whole being to be completely in love with Him. To trust Him enough that in the strangely uncertain, earthly times, the one thing we know for certain is His love for us. He wants us to practice being in His presence in the good times, so that during the bad times, our trust in Him is solidified. We still cry out and feel things. We still feel doubts, and we still feel scared. But we wrestle through it, and we come out knowing full well that *God is good.*

Humanly, our hope was that we were still being told he wasn't the sickest person in the hospital.

Ultimately, our hope was that whatever happened to our sweet son, either way, we would see him again because of eternal life through Jesus Christ. If Thao lived, we would bring him home and enjoy the rest of the days of his beautiful life. But if Thao died, he would be with Jesus, his Creator.

I couldn't be strong, but I didn't need to be. The Lord was our steadfast strength. Before this time with Thao, I thought I had to be the steadfast one in my relationship with Him. Now I understood, He is steadfast. *I am just falling into Him.* So I let myself cry as I read through more of Thao's favorite book. The quotes from this story pierced deep into my soul.

"Aslan is a lion—the Lion, the great Lion."
"Is he quite safe?"
"Safe?" said Mr. Beaver "Who said anything about safe?
'Course he isn't safe. But he's good. He's the King, I tell you."
(C.S. Lewis, *The Lion, The Witch, and the Wardrobe*)

Later that Christmas day, an officer from the sheriff's department stopped by. He told us they had heard of our situation, that they were praying for us, thinking of us, and that if we needed anything, to let them know. They knew we were two hours from home. They offered an escort in bad weather if we needed it. I was amazed at God providing the little things, like the support from these strangers, making us feel even more deeply encompassed by His love.

They handed me a dinosaur for Thao. He told me they had heard he liked dinosaurs. It was the exact one that Thao had asked for just one month before. I took it and smiled through tears. I couldn't wait for Thao to wake up and see this!

Even though I fought Christmas hard, my family brought gifts to the hospital waiting room. Jeff and I slipped out of Thao's room for a few moments to open presents with my siblings and our other children. Somehow, that created beautiful, bittersweet memories for Liam's first Christmas. It resonates deep within me. Christmas isn't always magical; it's just another day. The peace that Jesus brought to Earth as a baby, that is what I find magical about Christmas.

I didn't want life to go on without Thao. I wanted *everything* to stop. I wanted everything to stay the same.

I remember one person made a comment about Thao being so surprised to see how much Liam had grown when he finally got out of the hospital. It broke my heart, and I pushed the idea out of my head. I tried to keep Liam from doing too many new things.

We kept going, somehow. We managed to enjoy, embrace, and even remember the moments we had with the other kids during the stay in the hospital. We took turns staying with Thao and playing with Ava and Liam. We let everyone else take care of us. We made enormously scary decisions about tests and treatments.

But we weren't alone. The Lord guided every choice. He put an amazing team of doctors in our lives. I believe there were twelve or more each time we met together. He put nurses in our lives who went out of their way on days off to visit, to bring gifts to Thao or to us. They asked us questions about Thao and listened to our stories. Thao's room was covered in notes from his friends and pictures of our family. They often told us they and their families were praying for us. We gave them Thao's picture and permission to share. They reveled in his pictures and his interests. They grew to love our sweet Thao. They fought hard for him.

One day, one of our favorite doctors came to check on Thao. He told us how desperately he wanted to make Thao better, how he just couldn't stop trying. He wasn't giving up.

"I would do anything, I just wish I knew what it was. If I could stand on my head and make him better, I'd stay that way," he said.

Seems a little silly now, but then, it really meant the world to me because it showed me our doctor's dedication and *hope*.

Life went on, whether we gave it permission to or not.

CHAPTER 5

Trust

I sat in his room and wrote this blog through tears the night before he died. I wanted so desperately to end it a different way. In my mind, I did. I still read it the way I wrote it in my mind that night.

Thursday, January 12, 2012
Thao's Mom

I wonder how many times he tried to swing from the light above the table. I wonder how many times he tried that I didn't catch him. I wonder how many sweet treats he has hidden around the house. I wonder where his best hiding places are. I wonder how many times he beat me in checkers. I wonder what would have happened if we would have tried to make "canned pear bread". I wonder how God could ever bless me so much from one sweet little boy. I wonder how long it will be until I can hold him again. I wonder what real life feels like. I wonder how long this will last. I wonder how God can give us so much peace and comfort and yet, still have more to give. I wonder if donuts really do taste better to Thao than to everyone else. I wonder why all animals have always loved Thao. I wonder how God could make Thao with such a gentle spirit *and* such strong will. I wonder how many times I will read *The Lion, the Witch, and the Wardrobe* reminiscing of the nights at home, listening to Jeff read it to the kids. I wonder if any of you know how to play "Hide and Tickle" or "Come Get Me" or puppies or dinosaurs or Narnia. I wonder if Catlin (or Scotland) needs another good policeman to fight bad animals.

I wonder what heaven is really like.

Our time in the hospital is a distant memory now. One of the first nights we were there, I remember another parent coming to visit our room. His teenage son had cancer. He told us, "Someday, we will all look back on this and remember the time we spent in the hospital. It won't seem so long then."

In some ways, he's right. Those five and a half weeks seem like a whirlwind. Like a sixty-second roller coaster that takes off so suddenly, twists, turns, and flips you upside-down so fast that you don't register the events until they are over. You slow down and pull into the part where you get out, you see all the faces of the people looking in at you, but you cannot explain what you experienced while you were away. Not really. Not to the depth that they would understand, the jolting, the sigh of relief at the bottom of the hill, just to have you thrown deep into a dark tunnel. But then you arrive safely at the end, forever changed, and the world looks familiar, but you see it differently now. Your experiences change your outlook, the way you analyze, the things you care about.

My roller coaster was the hospital and losing my precious son. So many people around me have ridden their own roller coaster of loss in one way or another. Sometimes, the loss roller coaster is addiction, death, divorce, or something not so visible, like past hurts and failures. In so many ways, all our lives have been shattered by something out of our control. My roller coaster opened my eyes to others' pain, and I lost a lot of concern for the things I had once treasured.

Someone could have told me my house burned down and there was nothing left. I wouldn't have cared one bit. Honestly, I may have been relieved to have one less thing to take care of.

The hospital made me still. I spent a lot of time in the quietness, reading to Thao, wondering, hoping, praying. But I never wondered if God was in control. I trusted God, and He was near. This roller coaster was a mess, though. There was a point I wanted off. I prayed that the Lord wouldn't drag anything out. As much as I loved Thao, I prayed the Lord's would be evident.

Yet, at the same time, I fought hard. I refused to let myself think about anything but Thao getting better. I dreamed of the day we would walk out of that hospital and our family would be reunited. I tried my best to answer Ava's questions, to provide a sense of stability.

I was praying during one of my sleepless nights when God so vividly asked me to give him Thao. To place my complete trust, everything in Him. To surrender all. Up until that point, I held on.

I refused to let go of Thao. I needed him. Suddenly, I realized how selfish I was. I was holding on so tight. I loved Thao, and I couldn't see past the now, this Earth. I thought that if God loved me, he would heal Thao. I thought that Thao's story would be told by Thao for years to come.

And that night, I realized that was *my* plan, but it may not be God's. I was selfishly holding on to Thao because I couldn't see the bigger picture. I realized that for years, parents had lost children, not because Jesus wasn't near, but because our world is fallen and sinful. Terrible things happen to children, to good people, to Christ followers. We are told to draw near. To hold fast to His love. To embrace the goodness. To let go of our earthly ideas. His love reaches us where we are and pulls us through. This world is not the end.

At 2:00 a.m., I went to the hospital. I had to tell Thao.

I stroked his hair, kissed his face. I whispered to him how selfish I was to ask him to fight. I reminded him of how much I loved him. But I couldn't ask him to fight if Jesus wanted him home. I told him how proud I was, how much I would miss him. And how much Jesus loved him. I told him things he already knew. I knew Jesus was close to him. He resonated peace from that hospital bed. He was close to Jesus.

Monday, January 9, 2012
I Love You THIS Much!

Favorite kids' book of ours—my kids have it memorized, seriously. I just read it to Thao. "I love you best, I love you most. I love you high, I love you low. I love you deep, I love you wide. *I love you this much."*

(Now go buy a copy of *I Love You THIS Much.*)

The night that changed our lives (okay, there are many, but the *one* that began this journey with Thao), I held him in the ER in Danville. I was about to leave him with Jeff so I could pack and meet them in Peoria. I held him, not wanting to let go. I asked him to tell me who loved him. He knew. I asked him how much. He knew. I squeezed once more and handed him to Jeff. I left the room, only to peek around the corner one more time to tell him how much I loved him. Thao winked. That sweet, reassuring, comfort that came from my Thao. God knew I needed that. May Thao feel God's loving arms today.

"And I pray that you, being rooted and established in love, may have power, together with all the Lord's holy people, to grasp how wide and long and high and deep is the love of Christ."

(Ephesians 3:17-18)

Days came and went. His diagnosis didn't mean much in the face of the fight. We didn't see an end in sight, but we didn't look that hard. We lived moment by moment. We had thousands of people praying for us. We had hundreds of people asking us what they could do for us. So many people shared how Thao had touched their lives.

My Thao.

He was bound to a bed, hooked up to dialysis and ECMO (a life-support machine used for his lungs), medicated, and not waking up. His body was still. Yet God was using him to touch thousands of lives worldwide.

I was in awe of God, thankful for His people, and learning to live a life of letting go. Of holding the things of this world loosely. Of longing for heaven.

I trimmed his nails. It was the only thing I could *do* to take care of him. Jeff and I celebrated our eighth anniversary in the hospital. Ava and Liam each grew a size.

There were normal things happening in the midst of crisis. But somehow, this crisis life warped into my normal.

The hospital was my home. The staff were my friends. Friends and family were my family's caretakers. Jeff and I slept little and prayed lots. We shared our story because it didn't belong to us. We pointed each other to Christ. We ate roast beef sandwiches every day.

Wednesday, January 4, 2012
Confession

Okay, I have a confession to make. Today, during rounds, I barely paid attention. I couldn't. I just couldn't stop looking at the x-ray and thanking God for air in Thao's lungs! As they were discussing all the ins and outs (literally, I mean they were talking about lines coming in and out of his little body), my mind wandered to a day not very long ago. I came into the hospital one morning to find him reaching his little hand out of the blanket so he could show me his remote-control helicopter. Jeff had to persuade him to do it (he doesn't like to do anything when he's cold), and he gave that "if I humor them, maybe they'll leave me alone" look. Maybe, just maybe, those days aren't too far away! They are trying to wean him off the ECMO slowly so that he's solely on the vent. Then my mind wandered again. *I wonder if I can convince him to get a gray or tiger-striped kitten instead of a white one?*

Also, just to be clear about my last post—I am far from perfect, but I want to make sure I don't have any regrets. I want to be sure that I don't put the things that matter off until tomorrow, because tomorrow may not come. I wanted to encourage you to do the same, whatever that may look like. For me, God started a work in my heart when Thao was just a baby, to treasure each moment and put off the things that didn't matter as much. Some days are more of a struggle than others, but that is when I remember I'm not alone. I can't do anything alone. So, I make myself some coffee and pray for God's perfect patience and peace for my day.

When I was pregnant with Liam, I prayed that God would give us exactly what our family needed. Looking back, it seems like a silly prayer in a way. Why wouldn't God give us what we needed?

We don't always understand what it is that we need. In fact, most of the time, what I think I need is completely outside of the realm of what God knows I need.

Ava was always so independent, free-spirited, and smiley. She followed her Bubba around and was just happy with life.

Thao needed me more. He was always with us. He followed us around, helping, asking questions, discussing life.

As soon as Ava could scoot, she would scoot herself right into the playroom to play. Alone. She was happy as she could be.

I thought we needed a girl, a playmate for Ava. In my heart, I really believed we were having a boy, but I was worried about the dynamics. I was afraid I would somehow lose something special with Thao.

When Liam was born, though, I saw how God was working. The older two adored their baby brother. Thao was so gentle and protective of him. Ava was a little mother. Liam was set. He would probably never have to lift a finger, the way the two of them hovered over him.

God was making me more content than I knew possible. My dishes weren't done, but my heart was full. I was wondering if maybe our family was complete. I was finally learning how to live in the moment, to enjoy the long days, sleepless nights, and drink lots and lots of coffee. I knew it was a phase, but it was one that I never wanted to end. I knew how blessed I was and that the days with little ones were fleeting. I decided to treasure it with all my energy I had in me.

On Thao's fifth birthday, I cried. I mean, I *cried*. I was so sad my little man was growing up. My fears of losing part of the relationship I had with him were surfacing again. I was a planner, and I knew I only had thirteen years left with him.

Earlier that year, I had started my blog. I desperately wanted other moms to be encouraged. I wanted to share with them my triumphs and trials and point them to Christ. I started writing because I felt God leading me. I said yes. I didn't understand that God was preparing me for so much. This writing was just a tool that God used to start work in my heart. I used my blog to write down the memories, the stories of the everyday. I am so thankful for the minutes I used to write things down. I am thankful for the encouragement I receive through people that read my blog. I am thankful that God can use me, because I'm just a mom.

My relationship with Christ was growing through this new endeavor. I had a fresh boldness and passion in mothering. I passionately wanted to be still before God and be present with my family.

I connected with Thao very much when we were baking. He loved to bake. Most of our best conversations happened either in the car or in the kitchen. He loved to bake for other people, and he had a heart for giving. One day, as we were baking sweet treats for my grandparents, "Great Papas," our conversation went something like this:

Thao: "Great Papas are getting old, aren't they? They might die soon."

Me: "Well, yes, they are getting older. But—"

Thao: "It's okay, Mommy. They love Jesus. They will be in heaven when they die."

I'm thankful to have this fond memory of Thao's heart and soul. He knew truth, even at five. He knew Jesus because Jesus met him at a five-year-old level. The simplest of faith. The truest.

> "But Jesus called the children to him and said, 'Let the little children come to me, and do not hinder them, for the kingdom of God belongs to such as these. I tell you the truth, anyone who will not receive the kingdom of God like a little child will never enter it.'" (Luke 18:16-17)

I am thankful to still have my grandparents here. I've shared this story with them. It's comforting and thoughtful and true. And all of us are longing to be with Jesus, and to be reunited with our sweet Thao someday.

Sunday, January 1, 2012
There is never such a thing as too many pictures!

As I'm sitting here with all these quite lovely random thoughts running through my head, I feel compelled to share a couple things. I'm not sure I'm truly in the mood to write, but I don't want these things to be forgotten. I don't think I ever took for granted the time I had with my children at home. I am grateful to be able to stay home. I am proud to say my dishes weren't always done and my house was almost always covered in toys or projects. I'm okay with that.

I just want to encourage you to treasure the little things; soak it in; store it away; write it down; blog; take lots (and lots) of pictures; take pictures of the everyday, boring things; take pictures of their toes, their hands in yours, those beautiful eyelashes (that when mentioned always makes your little boy roll his eyes); take a picture of the eye roll; watch them sleep; snuggle; make play dough; create a new recipe; make a fort; go on adventures; make everyday an adventure; have a picnic inside; let them dress themselves (ties with T-shirts, boots in the summer, "church" shirts); hold them; kiss them (whether they like it or not!); fall asleep with them; consider their dreams.

I always say, "Someday, I'll miss this." Well, for me, that someday has come sooner than I ever expected. While I sit next to my Thao, I can't help but think back to our last day at home. My house was a wreck, but we got to watch Thao and Ava's favorite show, *America's Funniest Videos*, eat ice cream, and snuggle. Sure, I know there is a balance (sorry for those of you who had to look at my house!), but I am thankful God started working on my heart so long ago about my priorities. I'm so thankful God allowed me so much time to invest in my little ones.

47

I know that Thao has the peace that only Jesus can give him right now. I wish I could explain how comforting that is. I was reminded of this as I read his favorite Bible stories to him today: Jonah, David and Goliath, and Jesus on the Cross. Our God is *so* big!

One more random thought: I have prayed that Thao would have amazing friends to help him in his journey with Christ, to help lift him up, to be with, for many years now. If he only knew.

CHAPTER 6

A Moment

I really want this book to be so much about Thao's life rather than his death. Tragically, what you probably think of when you hear his name is something like, *Only five years old, his poor parents*, or if you had the privilege of knowing him, you might think of how much you miss him. If you followed our story at all, you might even think of dinosaurs or donuts or puppies, some of his favorite things.

My Thao was so much more. He was full of life. Unfortunately, it is more common for sad events to be burned into our brains. The news is full of scary events taking place in our real world, our neighborhoods, our lives. And somehow, we still have this mentality that it could never happen to us. Until it does.

Even Thao's life was born out of loss. Thao was not exactly part of our plan, cruel as that may sound. Jeff and I had been married a little more than a year when we started house hunting. After a few short months, we found the (cough, cough) "house of our dreams." Okay, really, our plan was to buy this cute fixer-upper and, well, fix it up. Together. Just the two of us. So romantic. So idealistic. So ... not gonna happen.

That first weekend, we stayed at our new home. It was beautiful. It was ours: mine, my husband's, and *surprise*! I found out I was pregnant.

We had been married for a year and a half by then. So really, we were just ahead of schedule. I always liked to be places early. This was okay. We were truly thrilled, nervous, excited. (But what you have to understand is, Jeff is way more patient than I am. We had planned on waiting five years before children, and I think he really believed that would happen.)

Two months later, we came home alone and in tears. Our dreams were crushed. We lost our baby, and I thought my heart, soul, and dreams had been ripped out of me. I was devastated. I was sad. I was a mess.

Jeff and I are best friends. Truly. We balance each other well. He's patient, strong, loyal, and fun. I'm not so patient, quite emotional, a little skeptical, and I like to play by the rules. I think chores *are* fun.

I had a really hard time moving past this miscarriage. It was all I thought about for a long time. I dwelled in the loss. Eventually, I learned that I had to make a choice. I had to choose to see the good in this heartache. So I did. I chose to see that every life matters and has purpose. We didn't know if our baby was a girl or a boy, but it didn't matter. We chose to name our baby Lucy, because we both thought it was a girl. Lucy means "little light." To us, this baby, our precious unborn child, changed us. She was light, a hope for future children, the start of a longing to be parents.

We changed our plan. And sweet Thao was born just one year later.

Jeffrey: God's peace
Thao: Gift of God

Jeffrey Thao Nardoni was born on August 25, 2006. He was wanted and loved. I was twenty-two; Jeff was twenty-three. Thao was born almost exactly one year after we had lost our little surprise baby. I was devastated by the loss; we both were. But that baby was also a little glimmer of hope. We could have babies. After we lost that dearly loved baby, we knew, despite the circumstances and our plan, that we wanted a baby.

My pregnancy with Thao included a range of emotions. I was still working, we were remodeling our new-to-us home, and I was terrified that little Thao would stop kicking. There were so many nights I would wake up and not feel him moving. So I poked and prodded, walked around, ate something, and *prayed* over this baby, until he moved again.

Thao was a stubborn little man. I was one week late and showing no signs of labor. He had his own timeline, even then. That morning he was born, though, I had lost all track of time. It didn't seem like forever, but I was focused. I wanted to hold my baby. And when my midwife placed him in my arms, he stared back at me. He was worth it. I will never forget Jeff leaning over Thao and I, tears streaming, and Thao just watching us. He seemed to look deep into my eyes. We finally met face to face. It was perfect; he was perfect. My round-faced little man.

I am thankful my sweet Thao lived me with for his entire five years.

Thao: "Daddy, what do you want to be when you grow up?"

Jeff: "I don't know yet, buddy."

Thao: "I want to be a nice policeman. You can be a farmer."

After some discussion, Jeff realized Thao wanted him to be a farmer because of the animals (of course!).

Thao: "Never mind, Daddy, you can be the nice policeman. I just want to stay home with Mommy forever."

Jeff: "You can live with Mommy and still be a policeman."

Thao: "No, I just want to stay with Mommy forever and do nothing."

I was seriously okay with this plan. I mean, I cannot really see Jeff as a farmer, but the part about Thao living with me forever was nothing short of ideal for me. Okay, maybe I wasn't okay with the "and do nothing" part, but this kid, he was our sidekick. Life with him was never lonely or boring.

I'll never forget the first time we left him to go out on a date. Our dear friends, his godparents, actually, kept him. He was seven months old. The cutest chubby baby, full of personality, but really, he just wanted to be with us. *All. The. Time.* Or was that me with him? Now I can't remember. Well, it doesn't matter. We all liked each other. He was an easy baby, so it wasn't difficult to just take him with us whenever we went out. Of course, sleeping was the real issue, but that's another story.

This particular day, I had prepped myself. We were going to take the plunge and leave him so we could go out on a date alone. I packed the bag, left a list of instructions. And off we went ... across the street ... to our favorite Chinese restaurant. We sat for probably forty-five minutes, talking about Thao.

And then we went back to get him. I was so extremely proud of myself. No panic attack. He was fine (of course). But I was so ready to see him again.

Like I said before, his life was born from loss. And I believe I was still grieving that loss. I also had dreamed of the day that I would have my own baby, for longer than I can remember. I wanted to soak it up. I didn't want to share *at all*.

For me, the worst part of giving birth was the fact that I had to share my baby. I couldn't protect him or selfishly keep all the smiles and snuggles to myself. He was a beautiful, fun baby. He was our gift.

This bond with him continued. Our love grew for him so much. Nothing could be better, except maybe two Thaos.

It hurt me to leave him when each of our other children was born. I wasn't as worried about Ava. She was more independent, more of a free spirit. Thao was sensitive, a planner, and a worrier. It still hurts so much to think about his struggles with friends, even at four and five years old. I struggled because I wanted to protect him. I struggled because I wanted desperately to fix it all for him. What I failed to realize was that he was content with the friends he had; our family was his safe place, and his Uncle Trey was his best friend. He was happy doing the things he loved, even though they were different from what other kids his age were doing. He was confident in his creativity. He was an old soul, a deep thinker. He only had conversations when it really meant something. He was thoughtful. These were all the things I am so thankful I learned to cherish. He wasn't the "classic kid," like my Liam is.

Thao enjoyed the moments he had. Thao taught us to slow down enough to soak up life in the moments. Thao taught us it was more about being together than playing with toys.

The days leading up to Thao's death were peaceful amidst the chaos of intensive care. Those days brought us to Jesus in a way I had never felt before—utterly broken, in a place that was not my own, where I had no control.

Thao was our son, but he did not belong to us. Somehow, along the way, I learned that God's love ran deeper than even mine could. That fact alone gave comfort beyond comprehension. And as much as it hurt to be in that place, I still long for it. I want to be that close to Jesus. I want him to be everything. Because once you've been there, that's all you want.

So when I was spending quiet time with Thao and Jeff was spending time with our other two, and the doctors told me there was nothing more, I didn't freak out. I didn't lose faith. I wasn't hopeless at all. I knew that either way, our Lord would be glorified.

My mind was going places like, Now *God will be glorified, because* He *can heal him when we humans give up hope.* And, *Thao is meeting Jesus soon. I want to be there.*

And things like reading Narnia and Bible stories. Running my fingers through his hair. Kissing his cheek. Holding his hand. These things were done with tears, hope, peace, and, somehow, joy.

Because as much as I wanted him to be whole again *here*, I wanted this dreadful battle to be over. I wanted to never see him in this bed again. I wanted my Thao back. I wanted my life back.

I wanted my family to be whole again, but I knew those days of climbing trees and traipsing through the woods with my boy were over. I was clinging to Christ, and I no longer saw just this earthly picture.

I read C.S. Lewis over and over again to my son, and recited Psalm 23 from the *Jesus Storybook Bible*. Through tears, I wondered if I was reading to comfort him or if he was the one comforting me.

His pudgy little fingers.

His beautiful, long eyelashes.

His wispy hair.

Jeff and I stayed up almost all night with him. Friends and family camped out in the waiting room.

The next morning, January 13, Jeff played Thao's favorite songs again for him. I got to hold my Thao for the first time in over a month.

As I sat there holding him for the last time, Jeff kneeling over us, gently kissing Thao's head, I was brought back to the first time I held him. Somehow, this terrible thing, saying good-bye to my son, was heartbreakingly beautiful. He was loved. He was cherished. He came into this world and was placed in my arms. We had praised the Lord for his birth. And five very full, short years later, we praised the Lord for the life he had lived.

I spoke words of reassurance to my Thao. Words he already knew. Jesus was close. We promised him we'd see him soon. He breathed some short breaths.

I remember feeling terribly guilty that I so badly wanted this to be over. The agony of holding my dying child, yet not wanting to let go. The beauty of being so close to heaven.

And from my arms to Jesus's arms, my Thao was gone from this Earth. He was suddenly with his Creator, the one who loved him enough to make him, sustain him, and pour deeply into his soul what life was truly about.

There are many days when I long for that moment. The moment I could still reach out and touch my child, the moment of holding a body when his soul is ushered into his Savior's arms. It's real. And that moment is a gift I will always treasure.

A gift, because I am thankful my Thao died in my arms, with his daddy's voice ringing in his ears.

A gift, because his life was fragile and there were many moments when we could have lost him, but this was the moment, and Jeff and I could both be there.

A gift, because no matter what, my Thao knew he was loved and fought for.

A gift, because that moment changed my perception of heaven and life and reality.

A gift, because every life is precious.

CHAPTER 7

Friends

"Thao is with Jesus now."

We uttered these words to our daughter. Ava was three years old, and Thao was her best friend, her Bubba. For so long, we had told her he was sick. We talked about him getting better. She asked when we'd all go home.

Four long weeks earlier, I sat with Thao in the hospital, talking about life. He convinced me to let him watch Spider-Man. I promised him a kitten.

Are you kidding me? When your child is that sick, you'll promise him the world on the day he walks out of there. For Thao, it was a barn, with goats and chickens and perhaps a peacock thrown in the mix. Yep. I rattled off a bunch of promises, with every intention of keeping them.

The first night, when we asked him if he wanted anything, he had asked for "all his puppies." So, my mom brought a laundry basket full of stuffed puppies. At home, we played puppies often. He was always rescuing them, comforting them, and nursing them back to health. I guess it was their turn to care for him now.

Word had spread that Thao loved puppies and dinosaurs in particular. Stuffed animals were his favorite. They poured in. Literally, from nurses, friends, family, strangers—this boy was loved. Sometimes, the puppies gave him comfort. Sometimes, they padded his legs or propped up his IVs. My boy was surrounded by puppies and a few soft dinos.

It made me think of all the times I would, against my better judgment, let another stuffed animal into our house. They always seemed so overpriced, and we had so many, but that didn't matter. They were all special to Thao. That's what he liked. Thao enjoyed going to garage sales with our family. One day in particular, I remember telling them we didn't need to spend any money on toys, just on things we need.

Thao was eyeing this little stuffed bulldog. He picked it up and snuggled it for a moment. I'm convinced his sweet smile and quiet demeanor could melt anyone's heart.

He walked away with that puppy. The little lady that lived there asked me if she could give it to him, and it made his day! We just added it to the pile that he kept on his bed. Every morning, he would arrange all his animals and often cover them with a blanket. Thankful for these special memories. Thankful for the Lord teaching me to slow down and enjoy them. Thankful for the moments I spent teaching Thao to make his bed. It really is the small things that bring treasured memories.

But here we are, placing each puppy in a bag or a box. Their job is done. Thao is with Jesus now.

Ava, of course, couldn't fully understand what we meant when we told her Thao was with Jesus. One night, five and a half weeks before, she went to bed, only to wake up with her family gone, her

58

best friend in the hospital, and everything she needed moved to a new house. Her stability became people, and only people. But yet, her best friend, her big Bubba, the one who promised to protect her, was gone.

She asked if Jesus might bring Thao to our home. She asked if we'd left him in the hospital. She asked if he would come back. Or if we could go to him.

The permanency of death is a mystery to all, but especially to a child who doesn't know it exists until it happens.

We desperately tried to explain. We calmly answered her questions. It was only by the grace of Jesus that she understood any of it. Of course, her simple faith was ultimately extraordinary as she began to take heart the words of scripture, the promise of heaven, the peace of Christ. Faith like a child.

As the days went on, we started to realize what a comfort our children were to us, but also what a long road we had ahead.

The waiting room was full of family and friends. For hours, they waited and prayed. I'm sure they paced and comforted each other. I'm sure every time the door opened, they jumped. I'm sure the wait was intense, because the end was near.

We knew Thao's life here on Earth was nearing the end, but as I held him, as I felt his last breath, I truly believed that God could have healed him. I envisioned God working a miracle and my boy breathing.

But that wasn't the plan. And now we were in the room, where we had once formulated a treatment plan, where we made decisions for his life, where we fought death and asked questions. I remember a lingering darkness in the room then. Maybe it was the time of day (because at that point, I had no concept of mornings or nights), or maybe the curtains were pulled. I'm not sure, but that day was different.

Where we once signed papers to fight for his life, we were now gathered to tell family and friends he had surrendered to death. This time, the room was bright and sunny, reminding me of our true hope, the one who conquered death itself. Other people cried. We ate donuts. We celebrated his life.

Still, everyone around me cried and hugged. And I sat there. Holding my other children. Watching. I had to tell my brother that his first nephew, this child that adored him, that declared him as his best friend, was gone.

I sat, watching. Unable to cry again. Unable to share in the tears or comfort. Part of me wanted it to go away. Part of me already longed for heaven. And yet part of me sat in disbelief, like I was watching these people grieve from the outside looking in.

He was my son. No, he *is* my son.

Jeff whispered to me, "Go hug your siblings."

Oh, yeah. That's what people do. They comfort *each other.* They help each other. They cry *together.* I wasn't sure how to do that. I forced myself to hug everyone. I forced myself to eat a doughnut. With sprinkles. I forced myself to smile. But the tears, now they were real. If only I could wish away the pain; it hurt to see them in pain.

At some point, Jeff and I made our way back to his room. It was silent now. The machines were gone. Every material possession that Thao had in those last five weeks was packed into boxes or bags:

puppies, toys, letters, cards, photos, a small Christmas tree, his Bible. Our still boy lay on the bed, no life left in him. His room was bright and sunny, calm and peaceful. I kissed his forehead, ruffled his hair, and we said good-bye to his sweet, small body.

I do remember at some point, Jeff called the funeral home. He was so brave. No one should ever have to call the funeral home to come get your son's precious body.

This is not where it ends. You see, Thao's life was a mere dash, a blip in the face of a lifetime. Five years is not a lot. But it was full. It was love. It changed my life forever, and maybe some of yours, too.

We found ourselves slowly leaving the hospital. People asked what we wanted, when we were going home. What was "home?"

I remember leaning against a friend, watching the snow. I felt frozen in time. I saw people crossing the streets, driving cars, going places. In a hurry. Didn't they know the world had just stopped? Didn't they care that my heart was just ripped open? Didn't they know my entire plan for life was shattered?

They didn't. I felt a lot lost. "What now?"

The answer: "I don't know."

Thankful for honest friends. Friends that will literally hold you up when you cannot hold yourself. Thankful for friendships that go miles, family that understands, and unspoken words. Because honestly, if words were spoken, I probably wouldn't have heard them anyway. To me, everything was near silent and still. I thought the world had stopped turning. I didn't know the sun would shine the next day.

But yet, in all of that, there was a consistent peace. At times, a relief, because he was no longer fighting. I was definitely thankful he didn't have to fight anymore. I was weary of the fight.

The night of his death.

Many people showed up. I'm not exactly sure how many, but many. All siblings, many cousins, friends. I do know that many of them stayed in the apartment with us. I just don't know how many or how they were fed. I honestly don't even care. It was distracting that they were there, but I just kept looking for him.

The kids were jumping on mattresses on the floor. Giggling. Playing. Their bodies were working. They called each other by name. All the cousins were together—except my Thao. Somehow, I felt like he was missing out.

If I only understood heaven, even a little, I would never feel that way. Ever. But my earthly mom guilt kicks in and hits hard.

My Thao didn't get to play with Ava or his cousins. He didn't get to see Liam crawl. Or camp out with everyone in this apartment. Or snuggle in bed with us. And he didn't get to stop for ice cream on the way home from the hospital, like I had promised him. A conversation that went much like this:

"On the way home, can we take Ava and Liam out for ice cream?" Shakes his head. Looks away. "Never mind. I don't know why I said that."

And my heart broke into a million tiny pieces.

"Yes, we will stop for ice cream, buddy; I promise."

And we did. Through tears. We took them out for ice cream. Because I'd promised. And in some ways, that's all I had left.

I don't ever remember doubting God's goodness while we were in the hospital. I'm not saying that I didn't wonder about things or ask questions; I just knew deep within that He was always and ultimately *good*. The Lord's arm reached around all of us; the peace was pouring out. But still, I wondered how it would end. I wondered how I would feel if I knew the ending. I remember at first, and especially on days when Thao's lung x-rays were getting better, I would feel bad for those parents that sat beside their dying child's bed with no hope. I remember aching for children whose parents were not next to their beds, because of choice, or fear, or events out of their control.

And then, there was a day I remember feeling jealous. I watched people walk out with their children. I watched cancer patients receive treatment. I watched as surgeries were successful and bodies were healed. And we were still waiting. So, although I never doubted God's goodness, I wondered when it would be my turn.

But we sat next to Thao day after day, his body quiet, the machines occasionally beeping. His blood pressure would fluctuate; his heart rate would bounce around. And I wondered when he would stabilize.

Something occurred to me. Thao was sick a lot. At home, we snuggled, watched movies, and hung out on the couch. He liked to sleep with his feet on Jeff or me. He often threw up food that he ate. We searched for many hours trying to figure out what was wrong. He threw up so often that the enamel on his teeth wore off, and just before his third birthday, he had four top teeth removed and crowns put on all his molars. He was sick. We took him to appointments, specialists, described his symptoms. They made notes, tested, and tried medicine.

He kept growing, though, although not as noticeably as he had in the past. But he was happy. Mostly. Irritable sometimes. Strong-willed. Passionate. But most of my memories are of him enjoying life. Some of my memories are of him exerting that strong will. None of my memories are of him asking, "Why me?"

Thao, my sweet Thao. Maybe he silently asked. Maybe he wondered. But he never complained about being sick. Sometimes, he would just rest and watch everyone, but most times, he was just a kid. A quiet, curious, observant, deep, old soul wrapped up in a body that didn't always work well.

Friday, August 3, 2012
Be Joyful Always

This is more for my fading memories than anything. August is a hard month. I want to remember to focus on what really matters and not be consumed by sadness or despair.

For some reason, today, I am reminded of being envious of the cancer patients' parents. Can you even imagine being envious of having a child with cancer? I had those thoughts. Here's why, in my finite mind, I had those thoughts for a few seconds:

☐ They knew what they were fighting. The good, the bad, and the ugly. They knew the nastiness of cancer, but they knew cases of people that beat it.

☐ They were awake to comfort. I mean, the child, even though he or she couldn't comprehend the big, nasty cancer, could be seen being comforted by mom and dad. They could express how they wanted comfort.

I remember that time so vividly, I wanted that. I wanted to know I was comforting my child the way he wanted. Of course, I know cancer is bad, nasty, ugly, and just plain horrible. I don't wish for my child to have it. I also know that not all cancer goes away and that sometimes, you cannot comfort your child.

Even though Thao didn't win his fight with HLH and HUS, even though he couldn't always respond to our comforting, the memory of the comforting is more for us now, holding him, reading to him, running my fingers through his hair. The perfect comforter brings those memories to light when I need them. When I need to work through them. And even though, in our eyes, we lost, God knew. God *knows.* God is good. Thao may have lost to HLH, but he has victory in Jesus.

"Be joyful always; pray continually; give thanks in all circumstances, for this is God's will for you in Christ Jesus." (2 Thessalonians 5:16-18)

CHAPTER 8

The Church

"At least I know where he is." I spoke these words often as people came to visit Thao in the hospital. I could think of a dozen things worse than what was happening. Although, and I know this is hard to imagine, I kept a running list of things I was thankful for. I still look back on this list. It takes me to that place again—of what's really most important, of being so close to Jesus that there's no other place you'd rather be. It's hard to imagine if you haven't been through it. I pray you can get there without an experience such as this, but honestly, once you've been to that place of pure brokenness and experienced Jesus as holy and honest and as the only thing, that's all you want. To be in this place. Again and forever. The earthly things seem to fade before your eyes, material possessions crumble, and heaven feels so real and close that you long for it, like you used to long for your bed on a tired day. I am thankful I still know.

I really felt like I was entering into a foreign culture when real life started to force its way into my day again. Thao passed away on a Friday. Saturday, we slowly made our way home, wherever that was.

We parked. We walked inside. I felt like I was a visitor, watching from the outside, or maybe a movie. It didn't feel like home anymore. Plus, it was clean. And let me tell you, with three kids, homeschooling, preparing for the holidays, and having a sick kid, we left our house anything *but* clean.

Friends and family piled our things inside. I walked around in circles. Observing. Wondering what to *do*. I wanted everyone out, but I didn't want to be alone. We were lost. We were wandering. Ava asked where our dog was. (With friends.) She asked again if Jesus would drop Thao off. *Catch my breath. Answer gently. Repeat.*

My grandparents came. I hadn't seen them since they'd visited Thao a few weeks before. They stayed home and supported, prayed, and helped care for our house. They have always been a strong part of my life. My grandpa, the fixer. He always fixed my car, helped solve my problems, gave me very practical advice. My grandma, the helper. She was always alongside Grandpa. She prepared meals, cleaned the house, and taught me how to organize a closet. I sank in Grandpa's arms. I knew this wasn't the way it was supposed to be. I had cried, with Jeff, to Jeff. With a few friends. But mostly, I stayed strong in front of other people. It's uncomfortable. How do they comfort me? They can't. But I sank into Grandpa.

And through tears. "I'm so sorry, Tiffany."

"I know."

The kids and I had spent a lot of time at their house over the summers and that fall. Thao's favorite place was their beautiful property, where he loved to explore. We took advantage of the nice weather as often as we could, hiking, camping (on occasion!), and riding bikes. Thao would find all kinds of treasures, rescue caterpillars, and climb trees. It was truly only a few weeks before

Thao fell ill that we had been out there riding on Grandma's new (slow-moving) three-wheeled scooter. I always thought Thao looked like Grandpa.

The days that followed Thao's death are quite a blur. Much like a wedding, but with less planning and more people. Or maybe not more people, but more people with questions that you cannot answer.

My mom told me people would gather. It never occurred to me that people would want to do that. I thought it was pretty normal for me to want the quiet, only a few people, but yet never be alone. So I think they gathered at her house. Or somewhere. They mostly trickled in at my house. That's how I wanted it.

Jeff and I met with the funeral director. I'm not quite sure who watched Ava and Liam, but I know they weren't with us. Our dear friends went with us, one of whom also happens to be our pastor, so that worked out well. They were solid. I mean, when we were in Peoria and there was a blizzard, we called, and they came. They answered questions and made phone calls. They left their kids with friends and scrapped their Christmas plans. You all need Kurts and Kimberlys in your life.

One of Thao's doctors told us we were the richest people he had ever met. He had met a lot of people. I do not know if he was a Christian or not. But he was right. Because he wasn't talking about money. He was talking about people.

I could make a list of people that you need in your life besides the obvious family (moms and dads, siblings, grandparents; you need them, but they ache too and may not be thinking clearly either). You also need Joshes and Joys, who leave everything to drive twelve hours overnight and move their family into an apartment to make sure your children are cared for, to do your laundry and force food down your throat. You need friends that visit on Christmas. You need friends that fly across the country just to be a face.

You need real friends. Friends that tell you bluntly, friends that listen. Friends that drop everything so you're not alone or play music for a funeral or buy donuts. Friends that arrange meals for three months because they know you lost your kitchen helper. Friends that leave notes and send cards. Friends that drop everything. (Have I mentioned that?)

But most of all, friends that cry with you and point you right back to Christ. Because even after three years, I still need the friends who quietly listen and pray. Because that is all we can do sometimes. And that is okay.

So, we sat at the funeral home. We already had friends there. The man with the gentle voice sat at one end of the table, telling us we could take as much time with this as we needed. Looking back, I can see how this could have exploded. Jeff and I had never talked about a funeral for our child before. Emotions were raw and unexplored. Anything could have happened. A sweet friend that worked there handed us some tissues. Kurt and Kimberly were with us. Kurt was doing the funeral. I don't think we ever really asked him. We didn't need to.

The man with the gentle voice, well, he "does" funerals for a living. So he asked us questions. Simple enough. Kurt would do the message; Jeff would plan the music. He asked us where we wanted to have the service. Huh. We had three churches other than our own offer to have the funeral in their buildings.

I'm sorry, but to me, this was a gift, a blessing. We saw churches come together to pray for our son, and now they were offering to come together to help us celebrate his short life. This was the church. Thankful.

We opted for a church that was somewhat close to the gravesite. It was January in the Midwest, after all. Weather was unpredictable.

Then he asked us to fill out some questions for the obituary. I stared blankly at the form and quickly asked if I could write my own.

The Obituary.

Thao Nardoni

Jeffrey Thao Nardoni went to be with Jesus on Friday, January 13, 2012.

Thao (Tay-o) was born to Jeff and Tiffany Nardoni on August 25, 2006.

His mommy and daddy, sister, Ava, and brother, Liam, will miss him so much. He has always been the start of our day, our planner, our timekeeper, our helper. He certainly kept us on our toes. He was adventurous, curious, and inquisitive.

He loved exploring in the woods, finding "treasures," and climbing trees. He also loved checking the weather, watching for storms, and playing with Daddy in the rain. There was not a day that he did not play dinosaurs, puppies, "come get me," and "hide and tickle" with his sister.

He was our baker. He loved creating new recipes and baking for others. Just the thought and smell of sweet treats made his bright-blue eyes light up. Thao also loved school, reading to Liam, and snuggling with his dog, Jack-Jack.

When he grew up, he wanted to drive an ice cream truck and give away ice cream to everyone, calling himself "Thao the Nardoni."

Thao leaves behind so many friends, aunts, uncles, grandparents, cousins … he loved them all, and he knew exactly how much they loved him! Thao blessed us with so many beautiful memories—his laugh, his smile, his wink. His life was a five-year adventure, for him and for us, and we can't wait to join him in his newest and greatest adventure of all.

A Celebration of Life Service for Jeffrey Thao Nardoni will begin at 1:00 p.m. Friday, January 20, at CrossRoads Christian Church, with burial to be in Sunset Memorial Park following the service. Pastor Kurt Sovine has been asked by the family to officiate. Visitation for family and friends will be from 3:00-8:00 p.m. Thursday, January 19, at Sunset Funeral Home and Cremation Center, A Life Celebration Home. Thao's favorite toy was a stuffed animal. If you would like to donate a stuffed animal, in lieu of flowers, they may be brought to the funeral home, which in turn will be donated in

Thao's name to the children's hospital in Peoria. All other memorial donations may be made to Connexion Church in Danville.

Monday, January 13, 2014
The Start of our Day

He was the start of our day.

We had a rule. He could not go downstairs until 7:00 each morning. You see, if we let him get up earlier one day, it would be even earlier the next, and so on. Eventually, we just made the rule about 7:00. He would come in early most days and snuggle before then. Or there were other days when I would wake up in a panic because he hadn't come in, only to find that he was asleep with Jack (the dog) on his dog bed.

In the summer, he would often start out in pajamas and end up with only his underwear on. (Probably the only time he willingly wore underwear!) In the winter, he was often wearing his favorite pajamas, a plain yellow sleeper, well worn loved. They weren't soft on the outside, but they were on the inside, and that's what mattered! They were just worn enough that he could "skate" all over the floors. There was just enough room in them to stuff entire packages of crackers down the legs, only to be discovered later by me when I pulled them out of the laundry hamper. When I asked him why the legs of his jammies were filled with pieces of crackers, he simply responded, "Just in case I get hungry."

Things with him were logical and planned and mostly revolved around food. He ate at least a three-course breakfast, always eating the same things for a couple of weeks at a time before moving on to a new phase. He was very particular about the way things were. He really only liked the way I made his oatmeal (even though Jeff and I made it the same way, he was convinced mine was better, and I didn't argue!). We always watched one episode of *Curious George* with breakfast.

He is often still the start of my day. Sometimes, the first thought takes my breath away or makes my heart race, but I am practicing making it a good thing. Like, trying to remember with a smile Jack and Thao curled up on the floor next to me, or his little voice asking for more food. It is also a wonderful reminder that I *need* to start my day with Jesus. I cannot remember with joy or properly grieve with sadness, without leaning on Christ. I just cannot. I still can't think very far ahead, and it's still hard to fathom that two years have gone by. It's so brutally harsh; yet, I feel triumphant that I have survived (although not alone). But I am still living a life that hopefully points my children to Christ and hope and fills them with good memories and a stable childhood, despite the sadness that living in this world will bring.

I am so thankful for everyone that mentions him. For those that knew him or didn't, I am so thankful for your prayers and support. Just the fact that you take time to say something to us means so much. Thank you for not sheltering your children, but celebrating Thao's life with them. His life, every life, is something to celebrate. Today, we celebrate with dinosaurs and donuts, smiles through tears, and hopefully, many good memories.

CHAPTER 9

Protection

When I was almost nine months pregnant with Ava, my wonderful grandma came over to help me sort through and put away baby girl clothes. Our bedrooms are upstairs. The floors are wood, and the steep stairs are too. Thao was almost two years old at the time. He went up and down the stairs like a champ—most of the time. This particular day, he started going down, and as I watched, he slipped. He bumped and tumbled down the entire length of the stairs. My big, pregnant self was ready to jump down and be the cushion at the bottom so he would land on something soft (and big and awkward), but my grandma put her hand out and stopped me. And even though I know it was a few seconds of me watching him fall, the image is engrained in my mind. The feeling of hopelessness, helplessness. The fear of the unknown. What would I find at the end of this?

Thao was fine. He actually fell off the potty later that day and hurt himself worse than he did when he fell down the entire flight of stairs. I know God gave my grandma a sense of clarity and wisdom in that crisis. It was very likely that if I would have taken off to catch him, I would have fallen and made the whole situation a lot more of a mess. I could have brushed past her, but I didn't. I listened because I know my grandma. I know she loves me and Thao, and in that moment, God gave me her.

Sometime after that, Jeff and I purchased the nice gates that open and close, and we put one at the top and one at the bottom of the stairs. I haven't thought about that moment of Thao falling much. Until today, I was walking down the stairs and I vividly remember watching helplessly as my child's body tumbled down the stairs. The gate broke this week. The stairs suddenly look the same as they did that day, and I'm reminded how much God protects me. Not by gates or by people all the time, but by His overwhelming, unfailing love.

As the image replayed over and over in my head, the feeling of Thao's little body in my arms after his fall, the sigh of relief, the praise for his protection, I realized how much this happened in his life. As parents, we want to protect our children; we try the baby food before they eat it; we check the bath water to make sure the temperature is just right; we keep them home when they are sick.

But there are times when we just cannot protect them. We seemingly watch as they tumble down through life, unable to interject or pad their fall. As I sat next to Thao in the hospital, this is how I felt. The only comfort I could give him was my love. I couldn't pad the fall, or take away the pain. I only could give him extra blankets and a heater to warm the dialysis. I only could read to him, pray for him, and rub his soft little cheeks. I couldn't catch him or protect him.

"The LORD himself goes before you and will be with you; he will never leave you nor forsake you. Do not be afraid; do not be discouraged." (Deuteronomy 31:8)

It was pretty quiet in our house, with the exception of a few questions from Ava and Liam's quiet cry, we were just there. Going through the motions. Doing life best we knew how in between his death and the funeral. People brought food. They called. Left messages. Often, I didn't answer. I couldn't. What were they going to say? I didn't really want to talk about it. I politely said thank you, but inside, I was screaming. I was overwhelmed and in awe of the support and kind words but there were times when I just couldn't understand. It took me a long time to grasp the reality of his death. I had to keep reminding myself where he was, convince myself really, that he was safe and secure. Those days in between were a blur, but time stood still, as it often does when tragedy hits. We went through the motions of forced eating and crying ourselves to sleep. Thao's room that he shared with Ava was untouched. She longed to be in there but she didn't know how without her big brother to protect her and talk to her. I thought all this would change after we buried his body. For some reason, I thought that magically, after the funeral, we would just know what to do and how to live life again. So until then, we did what we needed to do. We had our list, we took it one moment at a time. We had grace for each other. We walked in circles and shared stories. We called friends to help us find clothes for the funeral. It was the last party I could throw for my Thao. I wanted it to be amazing.

As I silently ironed our best clothes, I remember tears steaming down my cheeks. Ava chose a new sparkly dress with a gray cardigan. Jeff bought a new plaid tie. I had lost so much weight in the hospital; I had to buy all new clothes. Liam wore one of Thao's old "church shirts." Thao loved dressing nice. He had a style all his own. He wanted to wear ties and church shirts with jeans and sandals, donning a fedora long before it was so popular. He had cool "old man" style, and he wore it confidently. He had asked for a pair of loafers for his fifth birthday. Obviously, we agreed. He had chosen his own clothes for a long time and he had done it well. He loved plaid and dinosaurs, and he made it all work.

Now, he was gone. And I was left to choose an outfit for him to be buried in. His last outfit for his last party. Thao wore a white church shirt with a plaid tie and jeans. But no one ever knew. And I could just picture the eye roll from him, because I'm sure something wasn't quite right with the ones I chose.

Just before Christmas, I had made the kids all new Christmas shirts to wear. For Thao's shirt, I made a dinosaur wearing a Santa hat. He gave me a half-hearted side grin.

"Don't you know I like T. rexes? That's a brachiosaurus. But I'll still wear it."

Well, I tried my best to choose clothes he would have approved of, but it didn't really matter anyway. I knew Thao's spirit was in heaven with Jesus and had a new body. He didn't need my meager attempts at earthly clothes anymore. It was hard to separate from my care-giving role. I really, really, really just wanted to *take care of my child.*

The flow of people seemed endless. I had mentally prepared as best I could, but physically, there was no way to prepare. We knew the visitation and line of people would be long. We expected it and were thankful for it. We had asked that people bring stuffed animals, Thao's favorite toy, to donate to the hospital instead of flowers. The funeral home we worked with was simply wonderful. They cared deeply and went above and beyond our expectations. When flowers and animals first started arriving at the funeral home, traditionally, they took pictures of each gift with a little name card so we could be sure to write thank-you notes. Really, it's because they understand that those days become a blur and later on, they know you'll look back and wish you could remember who gave and who came. Thankful for people that were one step ahead of us.

They didn't take photos for long, though. It ended up being too much. Literally, thousands of stuffed animals were donated. They quickly gave up trying to keep track. But they arranged them all around the funeral home so during the visitation, everyone could see. Thao touched many lives. We were so thankful that didn't end when his life did. Even the local sheriff's department collected animals to donate. I'm still in awe of the generosity of our community. I have no words.

I'm not certain how long we stood up, hugging people. But I am certain we were surrounded by God, by people God purposely placed in our lives. I am certain we felt loved and cared for. I am certain many people drove for hours to stand in line for more hours to then quickly share with us a story, a hug, and some tears. I am certain my arms ached from using my "hugging muscles" so much. I know there were some people that came before the visitation started and stayed until we told them to go home after everyone had left. I know there were people that made sure my Ava ate and that Liam was held. I know there was a friend that brought me the absolute biggest cherry Coke from Steak 'N Shake I've ever seen just because she wanted to *do* something.

All of this, the waiting, the tears, the driving, the providing—we knew we were cared for and loved. I honestly don't know what to say or do to ever repay these people for their kindness and support. I struggled to accept any of it at first, but at some point, I understood. I understood that God was the driving force behind it all. That even those people that may not know God, were used by Him in those days. That these people were my people, were *our* people. They had prayed their hearts and souls out for my child. They had sacrificed their time and money and emotions for my family. They had to choose to not protect their own children from the harsh reality of sickness and death. This was real. This was what Christ meant when he said to:

"Rejoice with those who rejoice; mourn with those who mourn." (Romans 12:15)

and

"Carry each other's burdens, and in this way you will fulfill the law of Christ." (Galatians 6:2)

and

"Love each other as I have loved you." (John 15:12b)

Yes, as we stood next to our son's casket, surrounded by his favorite things, we were being the recipients of people's love, as Christ told them to. I knew the Lord was sustaining us in these moments, but he was doing it greatly through our family, friends, and even strangers. The stories that people told us about how Thao had touched their lives, or the memories they shared, kept us smiling through the tears. We leaned on each other, but only because we had the friends surrounding us doing all the little things that probably seemed unnoticed. Perhaps you took out the trash for us or slipped Ava an extra cookie while I was crying in the corner with a friend; *thank you.* From the bottom of my heart, thank you. Because you did the little things, because you did the busy work, I was able to hold tight to my family and to rest in Jesus's arms without distraction. I was able to process and cry and laugh, because God put you in my life to do the "little things." There is never a way to repay that, but you showed me Jesus in those days. I just want you to know.

Today, it is snowing. It often snows in the Midwest, but to snow on March 27 is a little crazy. Crazy stuff happens in our world all the time. It snowed the day we buried Thao, but that wasn't the crazy part.

The crazy part was that we were burying our son.

We were laying his lifeless body down. We were celebrating his life. We were reliving memories. We were going home to the snow boots and snowsuits that he would never wear.

The funeral was so much a blur. I remember walking in and seeing the casket. It seemed as if it had shrunk overnight. He had seemed like such a big kid. He was so responsible and grown up— but now, looking back, seeing that small box carrying his body, covered in his favorite things. He was just my baby. And no matter how hard I tried, I couldn't protect him. His battle was over, and he won. He was fulfilled, full of joy, running with his Creator. And it wasn't right or fair or anything. But it was. And so, we celebrated his life the best way we could.

I don't remember much. I remember lots of people, but even that was all a blur. I have no idea who came and who didn't. I remember someone saying something about five hundred people. I will never know who to thank and who to remember that day, because the book was placed at the front entrance of the church, and most people used the side entrance. I like to think it's because they were all family. Family doesn't have to use the front door. Friends and family don't always check in; they help themselves to the tea in your fridge. Thao's friends and family gathered that day to celebrate and remember his life.

I remember Kurt speaking the perfect message. Thao's life was honored and given meaning. Stories were filtered into the message about Christ and death and hope and heaven. Stories that bring joy in the midst of the hard things in this broken world. Children were pulled out of school to attend their friend's funeral. Sickness overtook his body, but he did not lose. We remembered this as we laughed at the stories of Thao reenacting *The Chronicles of Narnia* and assigning each of us a part. (I was the White Witch—always).

We smiled at the mention of Thao telling us that we misspelled his name when he was born. We listened as Kurt spoke about Thao accompanying Jeff to worship practice on Sunday mornings, always armed with a snack. And then he got sick. We lost the ability to parent as we had been, because the machines were taking over. The doctors tried to fix his body. And there was nothing fair or just about it. And as Kurt told about how Thao went from my arms into the arms of Jesus ...

I closed my eyes. This was real. His blue eyes no longer sparkled in front of me. He was gone. It was over.

But there is hope. There is life after this. And because of Jesus, this unfair, sad, hurtful world will soon be just a memory. This life will fade. And even though we should not be burying a five-year-old who, just weeks before, was so full of life and dreams, whose mother, just months before, cried at the thought of only having thirteen years left, we know *who* to cling to. We sat and listened to God speak through Kurt.

And then, Jeff and I got up and worshiped our Lord. Together. I had never until that day had the privilege of standing on stage and worshiping alongside my husband. I am not a singer. But I wanted to sing, to praise my Jesus with my husband, through this storm. Together—that was important to me. Together, we brought this child into the world. And together, we fought so hard for him. *Together.* I felt like we needed to do this for Thao. Thao loved it when we were all together. Our Lord had never left us. There was undeniable peace in that hospital room, and I wanted to share and encourage others; this was not the time to give up on Jesus.

No, this was the time to cling to Him. And so, in front of everyone, I wanted nothing more than to show everyone there my commitment to praise the one who calms the storm. I knew it would be difficult; the little I did understand about the death of a child was overwhelmingly awful.

The time of praising Jesus with Jeff in front of everyone— praising Jesus for the life that we were blessed to be a part of every day for over five years is a sweet memory in the midst of the pain.

Praising Jesus because He loves us. Praising Jesus because He was all we had left, and He was all we needed. Being up there, I felt like I was surrounded by Jesus. I was in the midst of something bigger than myself. I was weak. He was strong. I should have been defeated. But He held me up.

And that is what I remember most about Thao's funeral: being wholly, solely, with Jesus.

The funeral was over. We had asked Thao's uncles to be the pallbearers. One by one, each uncle grabbed a part of the little casket. I watched as they carried him for the last time. I thought about all the times Thao had wrestled with Uncle Trey. All the sweet treats Uncle Brad had bribed him with. All the memories that were just that: memories. Every memory and I wondered, what if we would have known those were the lasts? Would we have played harder? Cared more? Listened deeper?

Thao was cherished and treasured. He was loved, and he loved others. He knew Jesus with childlike faith that I still admire. I'm not sure that knowing his lasts were his lasts would have made any difference in his life.

And then, we threw the last party we could for Thao. After the funeral and the graveside service, where we left his earthly body for the last time, we went back to the church and had a little celebration. We ate donuts and were surrounded by balloons, which made it a real party. We talked with friends and received hugs. We smiled again through tears and thanked people for coming. Friends had literally come from all over the country to be there, for one last hurrah. For a proper time of remembering a five-year-old that so strongly taught us about life.

Flapjack Friday is still a thing at our house. Since Thao died on a Friday and his funeral was on a Friday, naturally, the funeral dinner was Flapjack Friday.

I honestly don't even remember how it got started officially, but every Friday since Thao was four years old, we have had flapjacks. For a while, he even had a flapjack T-shirt that he wore for the event. He was my kitchen helper, so naturally, he helped make the flapjacks, the fruit, the bacon, and the eggs. We still love Flapjack Friday. It's a reminder of simple traditions, something to look forward to. A symbol of stability in the midst of chaos for me, because it still happens. We still eat flapjacks on Fridays because somehow, amidst the chaos and the crumbling, life still manages to go on. We have chosen to continue the fun family tradition because it reminds us of our Thao, his sweetness, his sweet tooth. It reminds me of my helper and his voice. Sometimes, it's just the simple act of eating a pancake that takes me back to the simpler days, when my entire family would sit around the table and eat a little pancake with syrup.

CHAPTER 10

Grace

Before the funeral, I sat in my rocking chair and scribbled words.

These were the last words about my son, his obituary. His life had ended. What did I want people to know? To remember? How could I sum up in these few short paragraphs what his life meant to me, to our family? How could I rightly show the gaping hole in our lives?

I have spent so much time in that rocking chair. I rocked all my babies in that chair. I nursed them. I held them as they cried. I comforted them when they were hurt. I prayed over their fevers, coughs, and sleepless nights.

But if that rocking chair burned up in a fire, I know life would go on. I know that the memory of Thao sitting sick in that chair in the last-ever home video of him would never leave my mind. I know that there are other, probably prettier chairs. I know that it's really just wood and some fabric to cushion the back. Somehow, along the way, I've lost all attachment to things. I barely moved anything in Thao's room for several months. Life keeps going.

People used to ask me how I even got out of bed each morning.

I never thought about doing anything else. To be honest, I hated getting into bed each night. I hated the quiet. I hated the stillness. I hated that I sometimes woke up out of a sound sleep thinking I heard Thao calling me in the night. I hate that I do this even three years later. I hate that I probably will do that the rest of my life.

After Thao died, I watched TV at night. I watched *The Dick Van Dyke Show* to fall asleep. And sometimes, it would be on all through the night, because there were nights I wouldn't ever really get to sleep. Not a real, refreshing sleep.

Most of the days following Thao's funeral were spent just wandering. I used to plan every part of my day, my life. Now, I wandered through it. I didn't plan, because I didn't know if I could handle doing what I planned to do. I didn't plan, because I quite frankly didn't have the capacity to do it anymore. I mentally couldn't even think about the week ahead, let alone the month or years.

Other people fed us for three months after Thao died. I let them. I wandered through my days anyway. I played with my kids. I read a lot. I spent time with family and looked at pictures. I cleaned. I organized. I got rid of a lot of stuff.

Stuff bogged me down. For so much of Thao's life, I chased stuff. Probably not the way you are thinking, but I always chased stuff to try to make my life easier. I chased it to organize better. I chased stuff to make my home comfortable. I became a slave to perfection. I desperately longed for a place for everything to belong. I wanted a neat house at the end of the day. I wanted the kids to play and have fun, but I was guilt-laden with the way our house was always messy. I let it go so often that it ended up building up in me and then exploding. So for days, we would play and get most of our "stuff" done, put away, etc. And then finally, one day, I would just lose it. I would yell that we couldn't live this way. I would blame them for not being grateful, for not taking care of their *stuff.* I would cry. I would make *them feel guilty for having fun.* And then I'd apologize, feel guilty, cry some more. And let it go again. It was a crazy, vicious cycle that kept going.

There were days I would graciously step over the piles of laundry. There were days when I would smile at the toys scattered all over my floors.

I meant all of it. I meant from the bottom of my heart that I wanted our home to be their home. I wanted my kids to own it as much as I did. I didn't know how much I expected out of them. I expected them to play. I expected them to learn. I expected them to behave. I expected them to put everything away every time, all the time, with a smile.

And then one day, as I yelled about how awful our house was, the sun was shining, and I yelled. I yelled that no one would play outside until the chores are done. And by chores, I know now that I meant perfection. I meant absolute, with no grace, perfection. And the list kept growing.

So I fed the baby and barked orders. Until I didn't. I walked in the kitchen to an empty dishwasher and dishes all put away. The napkins were put away. The towels were in the drawer.

Thao wanted to play outside, and he knew the only way to get it was to do my chores for me. So he did. And I realized I was pretty much stealing his childhood because I wanted everything to look nice. I was giving him shame instead of grace. I was ordering instead of servant-leading. I was miserably raising my children to feel as though they had to earn their childhood.

And I self-loathed.

Don't get me wrong; chores are still a part of our lives. We still have furniture to sit on and toys to play with.

Every day, though, I thank the Lord for showing me, before Thao died, that I was missing out. That I failed. That I needed Him, because without Jesus, *all* those failures would have stuck. Because I am just a regular mom trying too hard to get everything right.

And finally, when I saw those blue eyes trying so hard to please me, it all made sense. So, I stopped trying so hard. I adjusted my priorities. And I yelled a lot less. I gave grace because I received grace. I loved harder than I did before, because I realized I took it for granted that my children would always just know that I loved them.

I served them. Worked alongside them. Learned from them. I adjusted my attitude and my parenting to be more present.

And only by the grace of God, I started learning these lessons before I lost my son.

I failed him. I failed my son. I know this because I am human. I am messed up, mixed up, and the farthest thing from perfect. But Thao getting sick or Thao dying were not consequences to my failures.

Hear me.

Thao's sickness, Thao's death, were consequences of a fallen, sinful world. A world where children die, parents divorce, widows struggle to care for families, and orphans fight to live alone. Where cancer strikes and men lose jobs, a world where hurting people try to survive. Some people try to survive without hope or grace or love. Survivors. We are all survivors of this broken world. But some of us long to do more than survive. Some of us seek joy. Some of us find grace. Some of us, not despite the broken, failed world, but *because* of the broken, failed world, see our need for Jesus even more.

I yelled when I should have held him. I pushed him away when I should have pulled him close. I hovered when I should have let go. I spoke when I should have listened. I talked when I should have prayed. I overdid, controlled, pushed, pulled, and twisted my way through parenting. I still do.

I also asked Thao to forgive me. I prayed with him. I read parenting books and begged God to help me. I prayed for strength and wisdom. I cried for him. I prayed over him. I lost sleep, pleading to God for direction. I fasted for healing. I wasn't a perfect parent. I'm still not.

But I have no regrets. I have grace.

As much as I try to fight the guilt, to excuse my behaviors or blame other people, there are no words to cover it. It's still there when I try to hide it.

But I found the harder I try, the more failures I see—the more I should have done or not done. I could have controlled my tongue. I wish I would have held him more. If I could have just one more day ...

But no.

One more day with Thao wouldn't make me any less human. I fail with my other kids, even though I live the reality of losing a child. I push them away sometimes. I complain. I yell when I should listen. Because I'm human, and I fail.

The guilt can run deep, but the grace of God is deeper. And there, I lay my burdens. To Him who created me, loves me through my failures and put me in this place, to be a mom, to be ever needing Him.

I don't say this lightly. Mama guilt (parent guilt, really) can be paralyzing. My house is never clean enough, my dishes are chipped, and my meals could probably be a little bit healthier. I'm sure I could spend more time with my kids (even though I stay home), and I most definitely could use some help in the patience department.

I remember when Thao was three years old. It took me awhile to understand that even though he knew the right choice, he knew there were consequences to doing something wrong, to disobeying, he still sometimes chose what he wanted in the moment. Most of the time, the bad choice was sneaking into sweet treats. This continued into his fourth year. We had been playing in the backyard, and he needed to go potty. I sent him inside, but it was taking awhile, so I peeked in to check on him.

He was crouched on the kitchen floor, eating brownies out of a pan.

I was sad. Sad for him, sad for *me*! I loved baking with him, and even more so, I loved enjoying the sweet treats we made together. He was always so proud; his eyes would light up. He had a passion for sugar. And I enjoyed sharing that with him. So when he chose this, I sometimes took it personally. I felt like he was choosing that over me. Because his consequence punished me too, I didn't get to spend time with him doing something we loved. And his consequence for sneaking sweet treats was that he lost sweet treats for a while. The first offense was usually a day; the second was two days, etc.

I remember looking at his brownie-crumbed face and asking, "Why, buddy? You know the consequence."

He shrugged his shoulders. "It was worth it."

Sometimes, even as a mom, I do that. I make a bad choice, knowing full well my consequence. I don't care, because in the moment, I think it will be worth it. Somehow, I get twisted and confused, and I convince myself that I deserve to lash out, to shut down, push away, or just use my position as a parent to get what I want. Selfish. We are all so terribly selfish sometimes. It really has nothing to do with being three or four years old. It has everything to do with our sinful hearts.

And when Thao would sneak the sweet treats, he obviously was hoping he wouldn't get caught. But he wasn't thinking of me or the hurt it would cause; he only had one thing on his mind: satisfaction that came from consuming the sugary goodness.

CHAPTER 11

Jesus

I remember the first time I was alone in my house after Thao died. Where I once longed for a quiet house, to find a little break in the chaos, I now found myself alone, without choice. The quiet consumed me, overwhelmed me, and I couldn't breathe. The house was tidy; the dishes were done. I listened for footsteps or his small voice. I found some vitamins tucked in the couch, hidden by his small fingers when I thought he had swallowed them.

I remember looking around at all the things he had touched, played with, claimed as his own.

And I called my friend. I couldn't be alone. She dropped everything to be with me. To drink coffee and hear me cry. To distract me, or remind me, to just be.

Wednesday, April 18, 2012
A New Rhythm

At quiet time today, I sat down with Ava, only to find my iPod needed charged. I pulled up Pandora on the laptop and randomly chose Chris Tomlin. First song to come on was "I Will Rise," a song that reminds me of the peace and hope I have. A song that reminds me of Jesus overcoming death and a place of no more pain and suffering. Of course, I'm already missing my sidekick today. The second song that comes on: "Here I am to Worship," Thao's favorite.

I know people have tried to comfort me with, "It will get better over time." I know that brings comfort to some. But for me, it doesn't. I don't want it to hurt less. I want to remember every detail, including the pain of missing him. I want to remember the struggle, the daily reliance on Christ to care for my child. The blue eyes that sparkled when he teased me. The laughter. The wink when I left him in Jeff's arms at the Danville hospital. The way he sat up and crossed his legs under the blankets so he could watch movies and play with his helicopter in the hospital. His fight. I want to remember how he told me who loved him. And how much. I want to remember his voice telling me he loved Jesus that night we went to the hospital. I want to share him with everyone, but I want to keep him to myself.

I miss him; I always will. I long to experience the adventure with him. I treasure the moments that Ava talks about her memories with him. I smile through tears when Liam does something exactly like his big brother. I've contemplated the "right" words to say on here. There aren't any. Just like there aren't any "right" words for you to say to me to comfort me. My comfort is in Christ. My hope is in Christ. I cling to Him. I'm thankful that through His grace, Thao is not suffering. Thao was only in the hospital five weeks, not six months. I'm thankful God has prepared my heart for this. I'm thankful for that crazy special bond I had with my son. I'm thankful he was the kind of kid that wanted to do *everything* with us. I'm thankful we did.

I'm learning a new "normal." A normal that doesn't make sense. A normal where you burst into tears in those quiet times that catch you off guard. A life that doesn't go as planned. Things take your breath away. You find it hard to breath. You smile in memory. You forget. You wake up and remind yourself it's real. You go to bed, just to wake up two hours later. You pray. You memorize scripture. You find comfort in what matters. You let go. You find strength in Christ. You find peace in Christ. You wonder. You question. You doubt. You live. You love. You pray more. You try to find a new rhythm. You tell stories. You wonder if strangers can see the tears in your eyes when you're at the store. You remember everyone has his or her own pain. You struggle through the morning. You praise God for getting you through yet another day.

The big picture is overwhelming. It's stressful. It hurts. Moment by moment, God's grace is what I need. When I think about potentially how long I have to live on this earth without him, I have pain. My chest hurts. It stinks. Then I think about how that time is nothing to Christ, to Thao even. I remember my days are numbered, and what am I going to do with them?

Oh, so much to say! I have so many verses I'd like to share, some excerpts from some books and such. But right now, I'm snuggled on the couch with my sweet three-and-a-half-year-old. I refuse to get up, so those posts will follow.

Monday, January 14, 2013
One year later

Yep. It's been one whole year. My heart is overwhelmed today at this thought. How has it really been that long? Yet, some days, time drags on so long I don't think we'll ever see that sweet smile again. Sometimes, fear creeps in. Fear that I will forget his voice, his wispy hair, what made him laugh, the eye roll, the wink, his favorites, his passion. Sometimes, I still cannot sleep. But, like anything else, I can choose to see the blessings. I had five wonderful years with him. That, my friends, is a true blessing. Even on the days when the tears won't stop, when all I want is one of those crazy, spontaneous hugs on my leg (or even a puppy kiss), I want to choose to be thankful.

Thank you, friends, for walking this journey with us. Today, I feel distance between my days with Thao and my life now. It feels like two very real, yet very different lives. When we lost Thao, we also lost our "plan." Sometimes, I feel like I am wandering, seeking direction, yet spinning in circles trying to focus and live a "normal" life for my children, for myself, for my husband. It can be lonely to feel as if we are doing this together, yet alone. We have those days. Those days when even though we know better, we still feel lost, alone, and overcome by grief. We all do. How do we wake up each day? How do we keep living when things don't go according to our plan? We don't. He does. I am so thankful for my God, my King. The one who can lift me up, surround me in peace, and remind me that I don't have to do it in my strength, because I am weak, sad, and lonely, and He brings me strength and joy and surrounds me with amazing people to walk this journey with me.

There was indescribable peace in Thao's room at the hospital. Today, I am reminded of reading from the *Jesus Storybook Bible* by Sally Lloyd Jones to Thao while in the hospital, about God's Never Stopping, Never Giving Up, Unbreaking, Always and Forever Love.

(Stop now and go get a copy, and then read Psalm 23 and cry tears. What a wonderful way to describe to a child the Lord's protection, His love, His plan to make a beautiful place in heaven for us.)

I could never understand how one child could be so strong-willed and yet so peaceful at the same time. I cannot thank you all enough for your remembering our sweet boy's life at Royal Donut yesterday. Thao would have *loved* it.

I became so fearful of miscommunicating or leaving a piece of the story out that I froze. I stopped telling Thao's story. I put it all away, my computer, my notes, even my thoughts and excitement about seeing a book come to print.

Why do I fear? Why do I struggle? I have been wrestling with Christ. Why me, God? Who am I to speak these words? To share these thoughts? I'm not a writer.

But God has been pulling on my heart. "Trust me."

I'm to be at His feet right now. I don't know what the end of the book looks like yet. And I'm not supposed to. So, friends, hang in there with me. Follow me. Join me.

Because here we go—again. Because Thao was worth the fight.

Someone recently told me that I'll be "tough as nails" at the end of my journey. I get it. I do. But is that what I want? On the outside, tough as nails. As in, I know I can survive with Christ whatever this world may throw at me. But on the inside, broken. And that's exactly where I want to be: broken.

Broken for my Jesus. Broken-hearted for this world. I want to be at *His feet*, broken into a million tiny pieces. Because I know that is when I am close to him. There may be nothing wrong in my earthly life. Or I may have nothing left.

Either way, this is where I long to be. So completely dependent on my Heavenly Father, that nothing else matters.

So I continue to tell my story, not knowing the end, but trusting in the now.

God, use me.

Monday, October 28, 2013
Fighting for Joy

Two years ago, I was secure. I was content. I was adjusting to my three kids. I was balancing homeschool, family, and church. I had goals. Goals with my kids in school, in life, with Jesus. I had goals to move and goals to make things happen. I knew what I wanted and I had a plan to get there. I wanted it for my family, for Thao, for us. I lived safely within my four walls, with the door locked. Simply guarded, protected, and planned. I followed

Christ, prayed, and read my Bible. I did my thing, I wanted what was best for my family. I wanted what was safe.

And here I am.

Sometimes, I hate the quiet. The stillness of a house, the rhythmic sound of sleeping children, the dark, cold nights and the late-morning sun. The red, yellow, brown leaves gently swirling to the ground. Yes, sometimes, I hate the quiet. Sometimes, the darkness starts to close in, the cold starts to catch up, and the reality of life moving on is just all too much. Sometimes, between the snuggles and the screaming, I catch glimpses of my children growing up. And sometimes, I find myself in the quiet house, reminded of what would have been.

I find myself wanting more. More memories, more pictures, more time. How quickly time passes. But even more quickly, I lose focus. I get caught up in the what ifs, would have beens, or what's next.

I remember the me of two years past. I was truly content with my little family, my simple life. So much is different now. So much change. So much to give up, to get through, to survive. So much out of my control. So much out of my comfort box.

Here I am; two years has passed—no, flew by, dragged on, gone. Two years, and I'm still here. I've made it this far. I've lost my son, my goals, my dreams. And there I go again. Counting my loss.

It's so easy to lose focus. To remember the loss, the last, the hard times. I don't find joy in that, though. I want *joy*; I want peace; I want Christ. Over and over again, I have to give it up, turn it over to *Him* who holds it all. It really is a fight for joy.

And if I could do it all over again? I would pretty much do it the same. I can't change the past, but I want to *be changed* by it. Every mom I know talks about being more patient, listening more, playing more—there's always something. We all mess up, forget, lose our tempers, blame the wrong kid, make the wrong choice. Having no regrets doesn't mean perfection. More than a clean house, perfectly organized closets, and children clothed in matching outfits, I want my kids to know *joy in Christ*. I want them to know I love them, to feel safe, and to have a relationship with the Lord.

After we lost Thao, I remember telling Jeff that Thao made me just want more. More kids, more love. He was worth every tear, gray hair, wrinkle, and all the pain of loss. Even though we'll spend the rest of our lives missing him, he was worth it.

Can you imagine a love even greater than that? Being a parent helped me to understand the love of Christ so much more. Through my loss, I have known a depth of Christ's love I cannot explain. His perfect, unfailing love. His love that gets us through, His love that drove Him to send His Son for us. His love that is redeeming.

It's easy to play it safe, to take care of me and mine, to love me and mine. To lock the doors, to have a plan, to set goals and not waiver. But God is bigger than that. And sometimes, God wants us out of that comfort box that feels so warm and secure. Sometimes, God has bigger things for us.

I've had people say that after losing a child, they would just love the ones they have left. I think that's totally understandable. Safe.

This is where God has us. He is asking us to love more, to give more of ourselves, to fight for the children that He has chosen for us. And there is no place I'd rather be.

This season, I am challenged to want more true joy and real love. *More of Jesus.*

CHAPTER 12

Pressing On

Day after day, the sun came up. Ava and Liam needed fed and bathed. They had physical needs that we, as parents, had to meet for them. So we did. Some days, we went through the motions with less than perfect attitudes. Some days, we powered through; we needed to. Dishes needed washed; cars needed gas; lawns needed mowed. And then, other days, we looked at pictures and had picnics by Thao's grave. We did and still do our best to help Ava remember him—most of the time.

Honestly, guys. I say "most of the time" because there are days when I'm not doing so great. Yes, I've lost my son, and there are days when I don't want to think about that part of my life. I don't want to remember the hospital bed or the sound of the machines. I don't want to think about the gigantic hole in my life.

I cannot even fathom.

I don't want to face it. It's hard, and it, quite frankly, just sucks. It hurts. And it makes my heart and my head hurt. And I don't understand. And I don't want to talk about it. I want to talk about Thao. But not his death.

I want to remember like it was yesterday the time that Jeff, Thao, Ava, and I played fruit hockey in the living room. (It wasn't real fruit; I'm not that cool.)

I wish I had more stories. But I don't. So I tell you the same stories over and over again. And you smile and nod and pretend that you haven't heard it all before.

Guess what? I know I've already told you. I know you remember. But I don't have anything else. I want to be like you; I want to have more stories. I want to know what it would be like to have an eight-year-old.

And don't tell me that I will know someday, because Ava and Liam will turn eight at some point in their lives. Nope. That doesn't help, my dear, well-meaning friends. (Sorry.)

I want to know what eight-year-old Thao is like. Would be like. What would the stories be?

And I will never, ever verbalize this to you. Because I really don't want the pity. But I do want you to remember. I allow myself to cry when I see his friends if I feel like it. I push it away, but the deep sadness finds its way back.

I am okay with that.

So, I beg you, please be okay with it too. I need that.

Monday, September 30, 2013
<u>20 Months and Counting</u>

I feel like everywhere I turn today, I'm faced with my shattered dreams. My ideal, my expectation of what should and would be. Gone. It has been gone. He's been gone for over twenty months. How can it possibly be fall—again?

I remember those last fall days with Thao. I remember the sound of his nervous laughter when he climbed a tree. I remember how big and strong he felt, like a cheetah, he said. I remember the leaves crunching underfoot. I remember the bushels of apples. I remember the snuggles. I remember his voice.

But how can it be so long ago?

We made it through his birthday without him, again. It's like it's real now. Doing everything for the second time, without him.

Yet, it doesn't get easier. You just get better at doing life without being whole. I know people say time will heal. But time does not forget. So don't be fooled. I think of him all the time.

And even though I try to not think about what would have been, I see his friends growing. And it is painful. Please know it's not that I don't care or I am disinterested. Many times, it's me fighting back tears while you are telling me of your second grader's latest accomplishments or how fast he is growing or the teeth he has lost. Please don't stop. I want to celebrate every victory with you; it's just hard.

I know my reality is that I am piecing life back together, that I have a new normal, and that my life is good, only because of God. I know that the brokenness is temporary. I know that in Christ, I will get through my day. I am so thankful for my two children I have now, for my two children and for my husband who just happens to be my best friend. But that doesn't make me miss him any less. In fact, watching my others grow up with out him and even grow past what he did, is a whole new, very hard normal.

I covet your prayers for the coming months. Many new things, many memories.

"Now may the Lord of peace himself give you peace at all times and in every way. The Lord be with all of you." (2 Thessalonians 3:16)

Mother's Day 2012.

It was a beautiful, sunny day, and I was enjoying a donut picnic for breakfast before church.

I was surrounded by my children, watching Ava twirl in her dress, listening to Liam's sweet baby laughter. And tears were streaming down my cheeks.

I was having a picnic at Thao's grave. It was still fresh. The grass had not even started growing over his little casket. Dirt covered his casket, his body. And even though I knew his spirit, his smile, his personality were no longer there, I needed to be there.

It was really all for me. *I* wanted to feel as though I was including him. Ever since he died, really even while he was still in the hospital,

I couldn't begin to tell you the guilt I felt when, to me, we were leaving him out. I wanted my world to stop. I begged God to make time stand still. Or let Jesus come. Or just to make all this come undone—this terrible nightmare of losing my child. But I couldn't be mad or bitter; I wasn't even depressed. I was just so sad. This was my heart breaking.

I sat next to Thao's grave, watching the pinwheels blow in the wind. I wondered why I hadn't bought one when he was alive.

I pushed back the guilt and let the sadness ensue. I just needed this. To be here, close to all my children. But it wasn't the same. And it wasn't just the fact that Thao was gone. It was the fact that Ava was changing. She was thrown into a position in our family that she wasn't born into. She wasn't created as the oldest child. I didn't think it was fair (and it wasn't). And I honestly struggled parenting her. I hadn't realized that what pulled us to each other was Thao. She followed his lead in everything, and without him, she was lost. She was a wandering three-year-old whose world had just fallen apart. She lost her leader, her guide, her protector. And I had no idea what to do or how to play with her without him. I felt like she and I just kind of meandered through our days together. Trying to get to know the new us, trying to figure out what our life was supposed to look like without our guide and planner. It was a lot harder than I imagined it could be.

Thao was artistic and structured; he provided the plan. We pursued his interests. I had been doing school with him since he was three, in a very structured, but student-lead way, because he liked it. She was more the easygoing, free-spirited, "whatever I feel like doing" kind of kid. She is still a happy, twirling, singing little girl, but she lost her way for a while. So we spent many days watching the slideshow of Thao's pictures. Five years of life put into about an hour of memories and music. It was beautiful. And we watched it every day for about a year. I was terrified she would forget him. I was terrified *I* would forget him. So we clung to what we had, memories and pictures, stories that we tell over and over again.

I kept going because I knew I couldn't deny Liam the babyhood he deserved. When I was pregnant with Liam, Thao and I talked often about how we thought it was a boy. And after Liam was born, I remember the sweet conversations continued. Thao told me about all the things he wanted to teach Liam. Thao had just that summer discovered that he enjoyed playing baseball. So my nine-month-pregnant self was often seen out in the yard throwing a ball to my son. As soon as Liam was born, we discovered the Moby wrap. Liam loved it, and so did I! I could still do everything I wanted to with my big kids. I had been so afraid of missing out on special things with my big kids because of having a newborn again. All those fears were revoked when I saw how much Thao and Ava loved their baby brother. So life went on. But I knew that if Thao were still here with me, he would never allow me to miss out on anything that his baby brother would have done. After all, he needed someone to carry out his plan to teach him to play ball, hike in the woods, and discover worms.

And I knew I had to choose. I had to choose to be the parent I needed to be for my other children, while I grieved my oldest. I had to let myself cry and smile, laugh and tell stories that hurt. I had to force myself to cook and bake and plan birthday parties.

Time wasn't holding still like I wanted it to. Grass was growing, babies were being born, and my children were getting older. I had to embrace it or be left behind. I had to cherish it or have regrets. I had to be all in, and be the mom I needed to be, the mom I had tried to be for Thao, or I would miss the childhood of my other children. And I wasn't willing to lose that.

So I pressed on.

But I wasn't the only one grieving. Jeff and I have always worked so well together. It seems as though God perfectly orchestrated our emotions through it all. At my lowest points, Jeff was strong and could comfort me, and vice versa. There was more to it than that. During the first year, with each passing month, friends would text, call, or send a card. Real people asked real questions. Sometimes, I felt like we were being watched, but only by the most loving friends. Friends that made sure we ate real food and cried real tears. Friends that listened and never judged.

But ultimately, God got me through the first year (and following years) because I chose to let him. He placed the people in my life to keep me busy or set me straight when I needed it. He was—and still is—my healer and counselor.

Hear me, though. It was never easy. And I am so thankful for the amazing group of people that surround me, but if that were all I had, it wouldn't be enough. Only God is enough to pull me out of the deep valley. Only God is enough to bring joy into a mother's heart after losing a child. I am just thankful He gave me eyes to see it.

Thursday, February 13, 2014
Life with Liam: On Heaven

In April 2011, I wrote a blog. In it, I thanked the Lord that I had never had to explain the death of a sibling to my children. Then, nine months later, I did. And I still am.

Today, I had a conversation with Liam about his big brother. His sweet little two-and-a-half-year-old mind is trying to process so much. His brother, Thao, is in heaven. His brother, Crusoe, and sister, Isa, are in Africa. Mommy and Daddy are bringing them home. (And according to him, we are getting a baby, too. That's not our plan!)

Liam was looking at pictures. "That Liam, Mama. That Aya. That Thao!"

"Yes, buddy. Do you remember where Thao is?"

Liam does know. "Heaven, Mama. With Jesus. Go get him, Mama. Go get Thao?"

And then I realize. To him, heaven is no different than Africa. It's a faraway place, but the people don't come back. To him, Thao is as real as Crusoe and Isa. And I'm thankful for that. We talk about how much Thao adored him, his baby brother. We share a lot of stories. But right now, it's all just so far in his little mind. I am so proud of his understanding and his gentle questions awaiting answers.

I snuggled him a little more and said, "No, buddy. We can't bring him home again, but we will go to him someday. We will go to heaven and be with Jesus someday, buddy. We'll see him again."

Liam doesn't question. He's two. He accepts the facts, but he *remembers!* It's so amazing. He says,

"Otay, Mama. Go there? See Thao? Go heaven with Jesus tomorrow?"

Maybe, buddy. One of these "tomorrows," we'll be there. Forever.

CHAPTER 13

Healing

I don't really have a lot of *Why me?* moments. I struggled with *Why Thao?* But God answered me every time: "Why not? This world is broken and sinful. This is what sin looks like." And I knew it broke Jesus's heart, because He loved Thao so much. I also knew that I couldn't see the whole picture, and I couldn't understand. I wasn't supposed to. It wasn't my sin or Thao's sin that put Thao in that hospital bed. It's this fallen world, full of sickness and death and unfair things.

"But really, God, I *love* Thao so much. Why my sweet boy?"

And guess what God placed on my heart?

Other parents love their children too.

No way. No way do other parents love their children as much as I love mine. No way (don't judge) are their children as awesome as my Thao.

Yes. I created them. I love my created. I love my children.

You guys, I'm not saying God audibly spoke to me. I am telling you *I cried out*. I *screamed* at God, because it hurt more than I could even describe to you, to watch my son on so many machines. To not know whether or not he was in pain at times. To not be able to hold him and care for him. You guys, I screamed my heart out to God.

It's okay. He can take it. I did this often in the hospital. And in my bed. And in my car. And even after Thao died. And you know what I reconciled?

That no matter what happens, God loves us. That He cherishes us and He longs for us and He is good and He hurts for His children like parents hurt for their children. Like I hurt for my Thao, my God hurts for me.

There were so many days following Thao's death (and there still are) that I just beg Jesus to come. I *beg* Him to return for us, to end this misery and make it all better. I beg Jesus to redeem the world, to save us all from this earthly prison. I'm just so ready for Jesus to come, to lift up his people and bring heaven to earth.

And you know what happens when I beg him for these things? When I pour out my heart's cry to him? When I ask him why I have to live *so freaking long* without Thao?

He's not done with me yet.

As I write this, I am bawling. Because it stinks and it hurts, and I see pain all around me. I see abuse and neglect. I see grieving parents and widows. I see orphans and homeless people. I see earthquakes and house fires. I see sadness. I see hunger. And I just can't unsee it.

So as long as I have to live here on this earth with this Thao-sized hole in my heart, I have vowed to the Lord that I will make it worth it. I will do everything in my power—no, in God's power through me—to share the hope of Jesus. To do as Christ asks me to do. I will risk it all, love desperately, and cling to the cross.

Thursday, January 9, 2014
There is Healing

There is healing. I know there is. Let me tell you how I know.

December was a really difficult month for me. I was just covered in sadness. I enjoyed my children, tried to not get stressed-out with Christmas (and did a pretty good job!), but everything I did and said was under a film of sadness. And even though it was hard, it wasn't the first time I've found myself in a valley, and it definitely will not be the last. I don't often share the times before the joy finally comes back.

I don't often tell anyone the awful struggle there is before the sunrises at the end of the dark night. Sometimes, it feels like a reunion with the Lord, but He walked through it with me. Sometimes, it just feels like a never-ending tunnel of darkness. Even though I cannot *see* the light at the end of the tunnel, I *know* that it is there. Maybe to you, this sounds like a cycle that needs to stop, but I see it as healing. It's healing because each time I come out of the really hard sad place, I am a little farther into the light. I am reminded of fully relying on Christ. Life is full of valleys, and not just when you are grieving a loss of a loved one.

Part of my valley, which was the life I dreamed about, was a shattered mess. Part of my valley was the weather, the date, the time of year. Not one of these things could I control. Yet, I had this feeling that I should control them, or someone should, or maybe that they were controlling me. I kept fighting though. You know, that fight for joy that happens. So I cried out to God for the peace that I needed. It didn't come right away. I had to concede to patience. (Again? Sometimes I just want to scream out, "I've already learned this! Please, please teach me a different lesson." Oh, dear. Like I have learned something to perfection?) I realized, though, that I was healing more, I needed to allow God to work and let *Him* pull me out of this valley so deep, so sad.

Even through tears, I was genuinely happy for friends. I began to dream again, I mean really. I hadn't remembered dreaming since we lost Thao. I thought that was weird, but I also knew that I wasn't ever going to be myself again, so that was part of it. I used to have crazy dreams. I read about other people who lost children and then dreamed about them. I never did that. Ever. It made me kind of sad, but just part of it. My dreams are not of Thao, but of friends from my past. Which is okay too. I wake up in the night, and I can fall asleep without turning on the TV or being completely exhausted. This is healing. God is gently leading me up out of that valley. The sadness will always be there, because I lost my son.

The sadness of Crusoe and Isa not being home with me is temporary. And the season of Christmas will always be bittersweet. But do you see it? The hope. The healing. The amazing grace of God working through a dark place. And although I actually miss the feeling of closeness I had when I would look for him and harshly, gasping for breath, remember reality, I am thankful that the Lord is leading me to a place of remembering with joy. I want to remember to be thankful for the five years we had instead of being stuck in the sadness of loss. I want to remember the beauty of adoption, rather than grieve the loss of a picture-perfect family in the picture-perfect house that I thought I wanted. I am beyond excited to see our adoption through this year, but adoption does not come without pain. I want to learn how to rely on God for my deep sad times, because He is giving me two more little ones with a world of hurt on their shoulders. I cannot help them alone.

So, I guess if you are wondering where I've been—I've been in the valley, but God has been walking with me. I've been struggling through Christmas, with genuine smiles and laughter. I've been practicing self-control because my two-year-old and my five-year-old are testing me. (I want to yell back when they yell at me! Oh, goodness, help me! They. Are. Loud.) I've been replaying in my head the two days I had with my new kids, halfway across the world. I've been realizing how much I love them already. I've been refocusing, readjusting priorities, and recovering from holidays. I celebrated my ten-year anniversary with my love.

Being thankful is my way to praise God through the storms in life. Sometimes, being thankful is all we have the strength for. Sometimes, being thankful is how we have the strength to do the everyday.

"Be joyful always; pray continually; give thanks in all circumstances, for this is God's will for you in Christ Jesus." (1 Thessalonians 5:16-18)

"May God himself, the God of peace, sanctify you through and through." (1 Thessalonians 5:23a)

"Be joyful in hope, patient in affliction, faithful in prayer." (Romans 12:12)

Right after Thao died, I needed to go to his grave at least once a week. It was a need I had as a mother. As a mom, I felt like I was abandoning my child. I had a very difficult time separating myself from his fragile body. Because for over five years, I had carefully guarded his body. For nine months and seven days, I safely kept his body from harm while he grew inside mine. So the mindful separation of our bodies took a very real toll on me emotionally. My brain knew his spirit, his breath, his personality were no longer inside that precious body. But my heart and soul took awhile to catch up. If I missed a week, I felt terribly guilty. I wasn't protecting him. I needed to keep putting things on his grave so everyone could see how much he was missed. I found myself more than once shopping for clothes for him—only to be rudely and abruptly awakened from the dream, to find myself in this real reality of life without him.

I also fought the selfishness of keeping his grave for only me and my family. I hated the thought of other people going there without my knowledge or consent. I was protective, because that's all I knew from the moment he was born. I was always greedy with my children. I didn't know how to share him, even in his grave.

So I continued to take care of him the only way I knew how. I wanted to protect him, his life, his memories. So I went every week with fresh flowers. We'd picnic and play near his grave. His grave marker was unique, with his favorite dinosaur (a T. rex) and the quote from our favorite book, *I Love You THIS Much*. It still never seemed like enough. I fought family trips, or anything new. My heart was waiting for Thao. But my mind knew that day would never come again.

I battled this desire versus reality for several months. I allowed myself time to grieve, time to heal, but I kept pushing myself to move forward. Thao wouldn't have wanted me to stop. Thao embraced life. To stop doing this would be to fail. To stop living life with my other children and my amazing husband would be to give up on everything. It would be a wasted life.

We took our time in everything we did. We celebrated every birthday, but with a little less passion than we had before. Some things were forced. And some things were put off. I just didn't have the capacity to parent, to friend, to live the exact same way I had in the past. And that's okay. It's perfectly okay. To live the exact same way would be to ignore the changes in my life, and in a sense, ignoring God's work in my life. So I chose to embrace the changes with grace instead of regret.

Each day was and still is a new challenge. It took me six months to make cookies again. And let me tell you, it's still not easy. I allow myself to cry through it. Sometimes, I need to be surrounded by my people—and sometimes, I need to be alone. All the time, I need my Jesus, my counselor, my Savior, my comfort.

Marked in my Bible on March 1, 2012, seven weeks after losing Thao:

"He who dwells in the shelter of the Most High
will rest in the shadow of the Almighty.
I will say of the Lord, "He is my refuge and my fortress,
my God, in whom I trust." (Psalm 91:1–2)

CHAPTER 14

Dreaming

We had barely left the hospital for the last time when I remember telling Jeff that Thao just made me want ten more children.

This may seem odd to you (probably in more ways than one). Thao always made me want more. And even going through the illness, the unknowns and now living without him, it only makes me want to love more.

It makes me want to love more freely, more generously, more graciously. It makes me want to love more people. It makes me want to love the unloved.

Because as short as my sweet Thao's life was, it was full. He was loved, he experienced love, and he gave it away. We fulfilled our goals as parents; we loved him well; we did our best to guide and discipline him; we provided the most basic needs, such as food, water, and shelter; and most of all, we showed him Jesus.

Parenting is hard, y'all. I'm not at all saying we have been perfect parents, or that we have it all figured out. I'm just saying that basically, we trust Jesus; we listen and He guides; we cry out and He answers. Many times in parenting, that's all we have. I cringe when I think of

Liam playing sports someday or Ava going anywhere on her own. I want to hover, but I have to choose to trust. I have to let go when it's time, but until those times come (and they sneak up on you, I hear), I will just pour into them every moment I have. I will be a greedy parent, soaking up every ounce of time I have. I will focus on the quality time, not the quantity, and I will trust the Lord. I thought that being so desperate for my son's healing was the depth of my faith, but let me tell you, it's not death that we should fear, it's missing out on the life.

As I said before, I vowed to the Lord to not waste my days. I still mess up. I dawdle my time away some days. I wonder at times if I spoke truth into my children's hearts that day or if my motives were pure. I wonder if I'm teaching them to be humble servants or just plain selfish, like I am so often. I pray for wisdom, and I pray that I remember to make a conscious choice, but mostly, I just pray that they see Jesus, seek Him and that He draws near with grace to cover us all.

Through this, Jeff and I decided to pursue our dream of adoption. If we gained any earthly knowledge through losing our son, it's that we shouldn't wait until later to pursue dreams. Sometimes, there are things that are worth the risk; whether the risk is emotional, physical, or financial, some things are just worth it.

Children are worth the risk. Thao was worth the risk, worth the fight, and worth all the pain. Every child deserves to know that someone is fighting for him or her. Every child deserves a family. Every child deserves to know love.

Just a few short months after losing our son, we started a new journey. A journey of risk, a journey that always, always, always starts with loss. The journey of adoption.

June 26, 2012
A Time for Everything

I've been playing around with this blog for days now, in my head.

In case you are wondering, I think about him all the time. You won't hurt my feelings when you say his name. I miss him. I ache. You will see my smiles, laughter, and my ability to function in a normal routine again. I genuinely love and appreciate my life, and I am learning to live with that ache in my heart. I love to talk about him. You see, that is how I will remember him. My sweet, passionate boy will be part of my daily life forever. You will have to listen to my stories, my memories, because that is all I have of him. I will see him again. What seems like so long now, will be yet a blink then. The painful times will be the memory then.

You don't realize how quickly children grow until one isn't growing anymore. That thought is painful, yet comforting. Time is passing, and our time with Thao here on Earth is more distant. But my other two beautiful children are growing and learning about life with such excitement and wonder. As children grow all around me, Thao will forever be five in my mind. So, it's time to cherish these moments as Ava and Liam change a little each day. It's time to remember, through tears and a smile, our forever five-year-old. It's time to praise God, to cling to his promises. It's time to pray continually and live in Christ, each moment of the day. Thank you, Lord, for memories, sunshine, and a new day!

Ecclesiastes 3:1–8, 11

There is a time for everything, and a season for every activity under heaven:
a time to be born and a time to die,
a time to plant and a time to uproot,
a time to kill and a time to heal,
a time to tear down and a time to build,
a time to weep and a time to laugh,
a time to mourn and a time to dance,
a time to scatter stones and a time to gather them,
a time to embrace and a time to refrain,
a time to search and a time to give up,
a time to keep and a time to throw away,
a time to tear and a time to mend,
a time to be silent and a time to speak,
a time to love and a time to hate,
a time for war and a time for peace.
He has made everything beautiful in it's time. He has set eternity in the hearts of men; yet they cannot fathom what God has done from beginning to end.

There are still days when I want to throw myself on Thao's grave. I can just picture myself sprawled out, facedown, trying to cover his grave with my body.

And then having someone drive by and see the crazy lady that's facedown in the dirt at the cemetery. You are probably laughing, or maybe you are thinking I've completely lost my mind. I've also wanted to buy Easter clothes for him and leave them on his grave.

Or I've just wanted to be there. Sobbing my heart out, letting the tears fall onto his grave marker.

I've sat next to his grave, in the mud, watching the ants in the anthill on the bottom corner of his marker, doing what ants do. I've watched them in awe, and I think about how busy they are.

And I've thanked God for the ants that live on the corner of Thao's grave. I've thanked God for the fact that there is so much land surrounding Thao's grave. I've sat there and watched wild turkeys wandering around, and there are woods just a few yards away. His favorite place to explore.

You may think these are crazy thoughts, or that my thankful list is a way of coping. They are and it is, but it's a choice to see the light in the dark. It's a choice to let the sun shine down on my face and smile through tears, remembering how much I have to live for or all the times that Thao and I blew bubbles in that same sunshine.

Or maybe you understand. Maybe you've lost. Maybe it was a child, or the hope of a child. Maybe it was your spouse, or even your dreams for the life you thought you would have.

I just want you to know that you are not alone. We all wander through life sometimes, seeking to find our place, searching for that point when it all falls just right and all the ducks are in a row.

For me, it was just simply my family. I strived for contentment in my home, but I longed for a home in the country. I wanted it deeply for myself, but also for my Thao.

Thao wasn't saving his money for a new toy or a bike. At five years old, my Thao was saving his money for a barn, with chickens and goats and a peacock. I was often amazed at his way with animals. My strong-willed child was such a gentle spirit when it came to these critters. The mean goats, the skeptical old cats, the chicks, the protective pups—he had a way with them.

As parents, we meet our children's needs for food, shelter, and clothing. We do our best to encourage them, build them up emotionally, and challenge them spiritually. But when you are sitting next to your critically ill child, suddenly, nothing else matters to you. Yet there are moments of guilt for the material needs, the earthly desires of your child that you haven't fulfilled. And you realize that you may never get to.

So, whether by choice or not, we were not able to fulfill all of Thao's earthly goals.

It took me a long time to see any light in that darkness. I still have the envelope of his money that he was saving for his barn. Each time I see his name on it, my stomach drops. Of course, I wish that he would have lived long enough to have his own little farm, but I'm not sorry about this:

I let him dream. I let him have goals and a plan and desires, which sometimes were not like mine. I let him talk about it, and I tried to humbly encourage him. And for the longest time, I was determined to not fulfill those dreams without him. My dreams changed because my dreams were crushed, shattered when he died.

Even though Thao's dreams of saving hurt animals and giving ice cream away to everyone didn't come true, I am choosing joy in those memories. I can see the pure innocence of a child when I remember his dreams. I can dream again. In memory of him, because of him.

And if we ever move and buy a barn with chickens and goats and a peacock and white kitten, we will name them things like "Smoots" or "Newey" or "Aslan," because I'm just certain those are the names he would have chosen.

CHAPTER 15

Life

I'm not an expert on grief. I haven't studied it or counseled, but I am experiencing it. And one thing I know for sure is that no one can tell you how you will grieve. I can tell you that grief is unpredictable. I can tell you it's sometimes crippling. But I have no idea how you or your body will respond to the feelings of grief. We often misunderstand grief to only mean sadness due to the loss of a loved one. There are many things to grieve, though.

I have grieved the loss of babies through miscarriage, the loss of my sweet five-year-old boy, but I've also grieved the life I thought I would have had. I have grieved over babies I will never get to birth, a wedding and grandchildren that will never come to be. I have grieved over small, wood pop-gun toys and the fact that I will no longer find vitamins hidden inside my couch cushions. I have grieved time lost and time yet to come. Part of my identity is and forever will be, a grieving mother.

Because each milestone we miss with Thao becomes a new leg of my journey, another part of him, and his life to grieve.

I allow myself to grieve. I know that there is a time for mourning. I must allow myself to grieve, undeniably, or it will cripple my soul. If I don't allow myself to grieve, I won't have the capacity to enjoy my life with my husband or my other children. I only have one life, and I want to use it well. I allow myself the time to grieve, whatever that may look like, but I do that while searching scripture. I look into the heart of God to find comfort for my grief. Wasting my life is not an option.

But what exactly does it look like for me to not waste my life? How do I live well?

So many times, I want these answers to be in a burning bush with words audibly spoken by God himself. It doesn't usually happen that way for me, and quite honestly, I've been jealous of Moses more times than I can count. But I do know that when I seek Him, when I pour out my heart to Him, when I beg Him for answers, I find them.

Sometimes, the answers are to *be still.*

Sometimes, He asks me to do crazy things (write a book, perhaps?).

Sometimes, I have to get on my knees in my bedroom and beg Him for clarity, because I cannot believe the things He wants me to do. I'm small. I'm me. I'm just this one person, a mom, a wife, a friend.

All the time, though, He wants me to keep coming back to Him. To be near. To listen and obey. To glorify Him with my breath.

So while I do dishes and teach my children, make beds, and advocate for precious orphans, I will do so by remembering that as I serve these beautiful people around me, I am ultimately serving Christ. Because He created them. He loves them. He *knows* them.

It definitely doesn't make my role as a grieving parent any easier. It really doesn't get easier, and everyone that tells you it does either has superpowers, or I believe is not fully immersing themselves in the reality of loss (or maybe has not experienced a terrific kind of loss).

I say this because it has been well over three years now and I am still fighting the quiet. I am still aching in my heart. It is fall again, and the smells, the breeze, the clothes—they all remind me of that last pumpkin we carved and the last walk in the woods. It reminds me of how quickly time passes, which both saddens and comforts me.

I'm sad because my boy would have been nine years old now. I'm sad because my youngest is nearly the age Thao was when he got sick. I'm sad because we are ever getting nearer to the day that tips the scales, when he's been gone longer than we had him here.

Yet, I'm comforted, because each day that passes brings me closer to the day I will be reunited with Thao. The day that heaven becomes home and I am face to face with my Creator.

As I read through much of my writing, I see so many contradictions that may leave you wondering. You are not alone. I'm wondering, too. How can I feel these things that seem so opposite and yet so real at the same time? Or perhaps my grief is restricting me from thinking clearly? Or maybe I'm just tired.

Grief is contradictory. It allows you to love and miss someone or something, while trying to ease your pain. And so often, I don't allow myself to remember or listen to His voice, because I want to ease my own pain. I don't want to go there and deal with hurt. It's true and real and scary so much of the time. And there are times when I need that break. But mostly, I want to remember Thao's voice and touch. Mostly, I want to be comforted by Jesus. I am okay living in this broken place, because living self-sufficiently is scarier than dealing with grief and pain and anger.

I still wish I could watch my son's face light up at the sight of his bride. I never get to shed tears over his graduation. I have to watch as his friends' parents try to teach their children how to drive. I will never have grandchildren from Thao.

I could go on all day. Grief is weird, you guys. The triggers are a mystery, and the cycle is intense. I'm not an expert on grief, by any means. I've researched how children grieve. I've read the grim statistics on the survival of marriages after losing a child. I'm a grieving mother, who is constantly—and sometimes forcefully—finding comfort in Christ. So maybe, in some way, that makes me somewhat of an expert. I think it just makes me an expert on my own grief. Analyzing and understanding the cycle of my grief, the triggers and what I personally need to do to cope and heal. I just pray that this, my sharing my grief and *my hope* will somehow help someone, somewhere.

I just don't want you to believe the lie that you are alone. Or that some pit of despair is the end of all joy in your life. Or that your feelings are belittled in some way. Because we all fall and fail and feel desperate for hope at some point in our lives. We have the choice, though, to deal with it or push it away. We have the choice to turn to Christ or to push Him away.

The good thing is, even though we (I) many times have pushed Christ away, we can at any time come back to Him. He welcomes us with open arms, as His child. How incredible to think Jesus wants me to be near to Him just as I long to be near my Thao?

God we praise you for creating us, for loving us,
for forgiving us and being near to us.
Lord, help us all as we struggle through this existence here
on earth. This world is scary and often deceitfully lonely.

Please, Lord, give us strength and courage. We seek your wisdom, your comfort, your peace, your healing. Please place people in our lives to encourage us and lift us up. Help us to not grow weary, but to turn to you for breath, for life.

We love you, Lord.

In Jesus Name,

Amen.

CHAPTER 16

The Battle

At first, as I stumbled through life in my home of six years, everything seemed foreign. I no longer recognized the sounds or smells of my home. I sobbed myself to sleep each night. I watched Thao's favorite episodes of shows over and over. I distracted myself when I woke in the middle of the night by watching more TV or crying. Thao's stuffed puppies, which we once placed around him as comfort, were now catching my tears.

Now, over three years later, I am up again in the middle of the night doing many of those same things. I'm contemplating grief, my grief. I think about how, at this point in my life, when I am almost thirty-two years old, I own it. I know my life has been and will be full of things to grieve. I know that part of my identity and existence is being a grieving mother. I used to wonder when it would end. I often look to the next thing, or what to *do*. The truth, though, is that we often cannot move past these deep hurts. Sometimes, there isn't anything we can physically do to recover. Many times, at my lowest, my desperate, most helpless, most broken times, I am the absolute closest to Christ. These times, I often think the clearest. Life makes more sense when you realize you aren't living for this world.

The tragedies and inconveniences that we often grieve can consume us or push us to find truth. The truth is that Christ is near, all the time. The truth is that life is full of these spiritual battles and when we are in these places in life, we see them. The battle is so real, the choices are more clear, and Christ's presence is felt, His voice almost audibly playing inside my head.

Why does it take these broken, stripped away times in my life to be the closest to Christ?

Why must I wait for the spiritual battle to consume me, for the grief to overwhelm me? I thought that, after losing Thao, that was all I would grieve. The loss of my son.

Tonight, I woke up in the middle of the night and burst into tears because I miss the sound of his pop-gun. His laugh. The way he would arrange his most treasured possessions on his nightstand.

And I realized that I do this: I wait for the battle to come to me. I wait for grief to find me.

What if I didn't wait? What if I purposefully went into battle? What if I place myself, my most vulnerable emotions and feelings, into harm's way?

This is why we chose adoption after losing Thao. Because after losing Thao, when I should have shut down, when it would have been easier to just be content and raise my children, when the thing that makes the most sense is guarding my heart and my family from more hurt and heartbreak, we opened ourselves up to more. And let me tell you, none of it makes sense.

It's also not at all easy, and many days, it is not pleasant. It's a battle, a spiritual battle. It's a battle to show love to children thousands of miles away. It's a battle to trust the Lord with my children, here and there. It's a battle to trust that God is leading and I am hearing Him. I say this because I am human, and I have doubted at times the things that I was so sure God was telling me. I have doubted because they haven't worked out like I thought they would. I have doubted myself, but never God. I wonder if I make decisions based on feelings instead of hearing from God. I wonder and doubt and beat myself up. But then, when I go back to Christ with all these fears, raw and real, and I cry to Him:

He, once again, comforts me. I am reminded we do not know how each battle ends, *but we know who wins the war.*

We are called to go into battle. We are called to trust Him, with our lives, with our children, and even with the *way* we hear Him.

This world is not safe, and bad things happen. The Lord led us to two beautiful children in the Democratic Republic of Congo, Africa.

There is just so much to this story. There are ups and downs and more doubts and fears. I have been on my knees and most recently remembered that God asked us to step out in faith, for this next step. He never promised a happy earthly ending. Thao died. He was our precious, treasured son. He was loved and cherished. He was wanted. He knew love and could express his feelings. He had food and clothing and a bed to sleep in. Jeff and I lived and breathed that child. He was a part of each of us, but he was his own little person. He was a child of God. But he still got sick. He still died.

That, in no way, means he was loved any less. In no way did God fail him. In no way did his life mean any less.

I believe this whole-heartedly.

I also believe that in a fair world, all children would feel these things. In a perfect world, all parents would live to raise their children. In my dream world, children would feel loved and wanted and treasured. They would know that God created them for purpose and beauty.

But our world is not perfect. Parents make poor choices and hurt their children. Children are left alone to fend for themselves. And even worse, there are people that seek out these vulnerable children and harm them. There are children that don't understand what it means to feel a full belly. There are children that have never felt a mother's arms wrap around them, to promise to always love them and try their best to protect them.

There are children that have seen death and destruction. There are people that have accepted this as a way of life. We don't blame God for these things; we thank Him for the comfort and peace to get through them.

This often doesn't make sense to our earthly minds. I've resolved that we cannot fully comprehend the ways of God Almighty right now. Because right now, our minds and thought processes are flawed. We are part of this sinful world, yet called to be different. The difference is that we believe in the sovereignty of Christ. We believe that we are called to trust Him. We believe that ultimately, *He is the only good and perfect thing.* True goodness. We trust in Him, and we know that someday, all things will be good. But not earthly good, with flaws. Not good and comfortable, like a soft bed at the end of the day. *Perfectly good, with no flaws, no hunger, no pain.*

"He will wipe every tear from their eyes. There will be no more death or mourning or crying or pain, for the old order of things has passed away." (Revelation 21:4)

135

And we enter into this world with a different attitude. We go out without a fear of death, because we have the Lord on our side. We understand that these beautiful people are created by God, in His image and for the great purpose of glorifying Him. We understand that we truly can and should try to make a difference in this world, for Christ, while we are passing through.

And after losing a child that I poured everything into, I did not shut down. Instead, I felt compelled by Christ to risk it all again and again. Because the risk of loss and pain is so small compared to the joy of a child, the satisfaction of knowing I am doing what God has asked of me, the contentment of being fully dependent on the Lord.

Only five months after losing Thao, Jeff and I began to explore the option of adoption. Adoption was a dream we'd both had since we were young. At separate times in our lives, we were introduced to the beauty of adoption. At separate times, the dream began, a little seed planted. And over time, it grew …

> as I developed some health issues in high school
>   and while we were dating;
> as we were told we may not be able to have babies;
> as we experienced loss through our first precious
>   baby;
> as we grew in understanding about the orphan crisis
>   and abortion;
> and finally, as we lost our firstborn son.

As we chased this beautiful dream of adoption, we were also processing the fresh loss of our son. Nothing was easy. But the adoption process made sense. The paperwork was predictable. Offering a home and accepting a child in need as our own made sense to us. We understand loss. Loving a child not born of myself is not difficult for me. The search began.

We desired to go where we were needed most. Again, making the most sense out of the situation. Understanding we cannot make a dent in the international orphan crisis, but knowing each life matters. We first sought out foster care and then domestic adoption, but finally, in January 2013, we landed on the Democratic Republic of Congo.

Not physically, at least not yet. But merely a year after losing our precious Thao, striving to obey the Lord, staying sensitive to where we were needed.

Maybe that's it; maybe I just needed to be needed. But the push (or pull?) of the Lord was undeniable to us both. For reasons I cannot fully explain, neither foster care nor domestic adoption were the right fit for our family at that particular time.

I will not get into the needs of Congo here and now. Thankfully, we are in the age of the Internet, and you may search at your will. It will not take you long to figure out why we felt as though this beautiful country was where we felt our prayers were answered. There was a child in that country that needed us, and we needed him.

It has been almost three years since we first saw their photos. Their stories are for another time. But I will say, although we have not been able to bring them home yet, they are no less our children. Their photos and stories and personalities, their struggles and victories, their courage and fear, their hope and trust, have all brought me closer to Jesus.

And even though I still don't know how their stories in our lives end, I am thankful they are a part of it. Halfway around the world, there are two children living and breathing, eating and going to school and feeling loved and most of all, learning about Jesus. All because of Jesus.

All because Jesus did not give up on me, or my family, or Thao. All because this adoption thing is a magnificent picture of what Christ Jesus has done for us. He has adopted us as His own. He has sacrificed and loved and has been shamed and pained all for us. He loves us that much. To give it all, no matter what the loss.

So why didn't we just live a quiet life? Why did we risk again? What if they don't come home? What if we get hurt again?

They are worth it. I look at Thao's pictures and I know without a doubt that I'd do it all over again.

I think every child deserves the risk-it-all kind of love.

Follow God's example, therefore, as dearly loved children and walk
in the way of love, just as Christ loved us and gave himself up for
us as a fragrant offering and sacrifice to God. (Ephesians 5:1–2)

CHAPTER 17

God's Story

My life did not end when I lost my son. My will to live life to the fullest wavers. My strength gives out. And yes, sometimes, it still feels as though my life cannot possibly go on. The reality is that life does go on. My other children grow, and I keep breathing and waking each morning. There are times when it feels as though there is a rubber ball bouncing around inside my chest, my feelings are sporadic and irrational, and I do not know where to land.

I start to think that things like doors and toys and T-shirts matter. I start to lose focus. I begin to say words and feel things that truly contradict my hope. I let myself go down that path too many times. Thankfully, I am yanked back to the truth one way or another. Sometimes, my loving husband starts to ask me questions. Sometimes, I cry my irrational fears and thoughts to my friend. Other times, I am moved by God's spirit, convicted of my doubts. All times, I am humbled back to reality. The reality that I am still living, the Lord has sustained my life now, in this moment. And I must use it to glorify Him, or I am living without purpose.

So I do my best to glorify Him in my moments of weakness. And I search scripture. And I pray. And I memorize. And I am grateful. For promises and love and forgiveness and redemption. Redemption. Over and over again. The Lord redeems my fears and doubts and sin.

And He brings beauty from ashes. He renews my spirit. He reminds me of the fact that even though these past few years of living without Thao *feel* like forever, and even though I have and will continue to mess up, mix up, and completely fail …

He is still God.

He is not shocked off His throne. He has not and never will stop loving me. And someday …

He will make all things new.

And the pain, tears, suffering, longing, and waiting will not feel as though it lasted forever. It will seem like a blink of the eye. And eternity with Jesus will be my forever.

And Thao beat me there. And with bittersweet, happy tears, I pray that you, too, will come to know Jesus. Maybe through this book. Maybe through Thao's sweet five years on Earth. Maybe another way. But I hope that you can sincerely join me in believing that God is still good. Always. Forever.

> For God so loved the world that he gave his one and only Son, that whoever believes in him shall not perish but have eternal life. (John 3:16)

Come, Lord Jesus.

Then I saw "a new heaven and a new earth," for the first heaven and the first earth had passed away, and there was no longer any sea. I saw the Holy City, the new Jerusalem, coming down out of heaven from God, prepared as a bride beautifully dressed for her husband. And I heard a loud voice from the throne saying, "Look! God's dwelling place is now among the people, and he will dwell with them. They will be his people, and God himself will be with them and be their God. He will wipe every tear from their eyes. There will be no more death or mourning or crying or pain, for the old order of things has passed away."

He who was seated on the throne said, "I am making everything new!" Then he said, "Write this down, for these words are trustworthy and true." (Revelation 21:1-5)

Friday, July 13, 2012
Blessed

We are blessed. Truly, honestly, perfectly blessed by God's grace. I have felt God's love through and through today. Six months ago today, I held my Thao for the last time. Even now, it's hard to write, read, say. It's hard to believe. I still think of things to show him when he gets home, but then I remember. He *is* home. He is in a place so perfect, so beautiful, so completely amazing—I can just picture him saying, "Those things don't bother me anymore, Mama." He will never have to go to the doctor, or get a skinned knee, or feel embarrassed or feel pain. Ever. Again. Forever. He is laughing and playing. He knows joy, pure joy.

Even though it's so easy for us to focus on the pain here, I am, through God's grace, able to see past this part, this phase. I guess our life here on Earth is just a bunch of phases. Our phase of parenting Thao is over, but I will always be Thao's mom. Yes, we've all asked that question, "Why?" But, it's not mine to question, just as it's not mine to control. God is good, and he sees us through each moment, and that is what I need. I've seen God's love through all your words of encouragement today. I cannot begin to tell you how wonderful it is to be surrounded by people that remember, pray, and love us when we need it most. Thank you.

With that said, we are doing what we know to do. We have our moments, we cry, we rely on Christ, and we love the time we have with Ava and Liam. We are in a phase of being a family of four, watching our baby turn into a toddler, listening to Ava reminisce of times with Thao, learning what to do now. We've had to pick up the slack a little; Thao was such a wonderful helper. He fed the dog, sharpened the pencils, packed the diaper bag, helped us bake, and cleaned. He reminded us to buy birthday hats and helped pick out presents.

We are entering a new phase in our life as well: adoption. Adoption has always been on our hearts, in our dreams for "someday." We have prayed that

God would open or close doors, and he's done that
for us. We are still in the beginning phases of our
home study, but we are excited! We are praying for
God's leading and direction for us, our caseworker,
and the birth parents. We are praying for our baby
that we have yet to meet. Please pray with us!
Love you all.

Looking back, I see how God has used Thao's life to touch so many.
And for that, I am thankful. The thing is, it doesn't stop here. Thao's
life will be remembered here on earth. His body has been restored, and
his soul has been redeemed. He is with his Creator in heaven, a place
where we should all long to be. Even though his body, his earthly life
has ceased, he will forever be in our hearts. He will forever be in our
stories. And our children and grandchildren will know him because we
will forever be praising God for the life that we had with Thao.

And when our adopted children come home, we will teach them
of their brother. We will share with them his dreams, his love for his
siblings, and how his life brought us closer to knowing them.

It all started out of loss. Beautiful, bittersweet, the story doesn't
end when that phase of life did. The story is just a part of the journey
that we will carry with us.

Instead of asking God, "Why me?" I often find myself asking,
"Who am I?"

Who am I, to have been blessed enough to be Thao's mom?

Who am I, to be given such great responsibility as to parent these children?

Who am I, that you would ask me to tell others about you?

Who am I, to tell this story?

Who am I, to speak anything to anyone?

Lord, I am no one. Lord, I am nothing. Lord, I cannot do it … but, I will.

Because it's truly not my story; it's His, and He has asked me to do this thing. This thing that seems so great and beyond me, but so small in the grand scheme of life.

2 Corinthians 12:9 says: "My grace is sufficient for you, for my power is made perfect in weakness. There I will boast all the more gladly about my weaknesses, so that Christ's power may rest on me."

And there it is, friends. I'm weak, unstable, emotional, and pretty much just a mess.

But His grace is sufficient. He is strong. I pray my weaknesses, all throughout this book, will point you to the one who got me through. I pray that you see the thread of Jesus sewn into the words. I pray that you will be encouraged to say yes to Him.

Comfort from Christ

These are the verses that have been on my heart. I like the short, sweet promises that I can remember throughout the day! I pray this encourages someone today.

I have loved you with an everlasting love, I have drawn
you with loving kindness. (Jeremiah 31:3)

As a mother comforts her child, so I will
comfort you. (Isaiah 66:13)

For the joy of the Lord is your strength. (Nehemiah 8:10b)

Before I formed you in the womb I knew you, before
you were born I set you apart. (Jeremiah 1:5)

But as for me, I watch in hope for the Lord, I wait for
God my Savior; my God will hear me. (Micah 7:7)

Let love and faithfulness never leave you; bind them around your
neck, write them on the tablet of your heart. (Proverbs 3:3)

There is a time for everything,
and a season for every activity under the heavens:
a time to be born and a time to die,
a time to plant and a time to uproot,
a time to kill and a time to heal,
a time to tear down and a time to build,
a time to weep and a time to laugh,
a time to mourn and a time to dance,
a time to scatter stones and a time to gather them,
a time to embrace and a time to refrain from embracing,
a time to search and a time to give up,
a time to keep and a time to throw away,

a time to tear and a time to mend,

a time to be silent and a time to speak,

a time to love and a time to hate,

a time for war and a time for peace.

What do workers gain from their toil? I have seen the burden
God has laid on the human race. He has made everything
beautiful in its time. He has also set eternity in the human
heart; yet no one can fathom what God has done from beginning
to end. I know that there is nothing better for people than to
be happy and to do good while they live. That each of them
may eat and drink, and find satisfaction in all their toil—
this is the gift of God. I know that everything God does
will endure forever; nothing can be added to it and nothing
taken from it. God does it so that people will fear him.

Whatever is has already been,

and what will be has been before;

and God will call the past to account.

And I saw something else under the sun:

In the place of judgment—wickedness was there,

in the place of justice—wickedness was there.

I said to myself,

"God will bring into judgment

both the righteous and the wicked,

for there will be a time for every activity,

a time to judge every deed."

I also said to myself, "As for humans, God tests them so that
they may see that they are like the animals. Surely the fate of
human beings is like that of the animals; the same fate awaits
them both: As one dies, so dies the other. All have the same

breath; humans have no advantage over animals. Everything is
meaningless. All go to the same place; all come from dust, and
to dust all return. Who knows if the human spirit rises upward
and if the spirit of the animal goes down into the earth?"
So I saw that there is nothing better for a person than to enjoy
their work, because that is their lot. For who can bring them
to see what will happen after them? (Ecclesiastes 3:1-22)

Be joyful always; pray continually; give thanks in all
circumstances; for this is God's will for you in Christ Jesus. (1
Thessalonians 5:16–18)

Brothers, we do not want you to be ignorant about those who fall
asleep or to grieve like the rest of men, who have no hope. We
believe that Jesus died and rose again ... Therefore encourage
each other with these words. (1 Thessalonians 4:13–14a, 18)

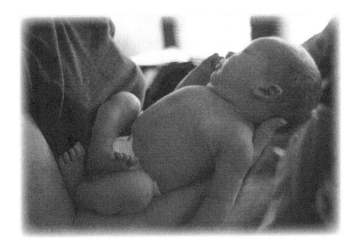

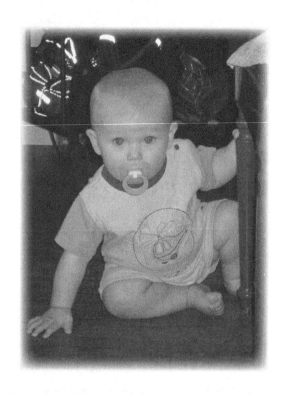

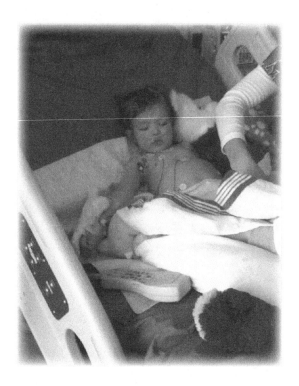

Notes from the Hospital
December 12, 2011

We talked to the kidney specialist this morning. He said Thao's doing great. They are going to leave him on dialysis at least another day, which means his body is handling it really well. Some of his levels that were really high are now down to normal levels. Over a couple of days, his urine level was twenty-one, and overnight, it rose to forty-one, which means his kidneys are trying to their job. They decreased the flow this morning of the dialysis machine this morning to see how much more his kidneys will do on their own.

His platelet count went down, from twenty to fourteen. I think they said normal is 120, but they said that is not uncommon with

Hemalytic Uremic Syndrome (HUS). Right now, we are focusing on this being the problem with his kidneys. As we said before, they are still looking for the cause. The syndrome is just a group of symptoms. If his platelet count goes below ten, they will increase his platelet count through transfusion. They don't wait to add fluid right now because his body is still creating it, but it's just not flowing because his kidneys are not functioning.

His white blood cell count is down, making him more prone to infection. We need to wear masks in the room and limit traffic to protect him from illness. We just wanted you to know that just in case you visit over the weekend, there is no guarantee you will see him. With that, please just pray that he remains free from infection and that there will be no bleeding. These things could very much complicate the situation.

The doctors and nurses have been so encouraging and helpful. Pray God for his amazing orchestration.

Also, Thao may get to eat if they can bring the blood pressure machine down. I think he would really like that. It might help him relax a little. He got to watch *Looney Tunes* today, which made him pretty happy. I also told him about his friends sending presents and that they all say hi and they've been praying for him. His eyes got really big. Thank you guys so much. He said he'll open them later on. I can't tell you how much you all mean to us. It's amazing the peace that comes with knowing so many people are praying and so many of you love our son this much. I'll keep posting stuff to pray for, and we're soon going to make a list of all the ways God has moved so you can see what we see. For Him to be known! Always for that.

-Jeff

December 13, 2011

Like everything! Thao had a good day today. He will be continuing on dialysis through tomorrow. It sounds like this will definitely be the last day of the twenty-four-hour machine. He started off the morning not having to be on his antibiotic or epinephrine. It continues to look good! Because they were able to stop the epi, he was able to eat today. He only had a little bit of vanilla pudding, but I'm pretty sure he was really happy to be able to have even that. All of his vitals are great, and all of his levels in his blood are normalizing. His phosphorous was still low, so they added some stuff to his diet and dialysis machine. His blood pressure is higher than normal, but the kidney specialist said that's good because it forces the blood and urine to his kidneys to get them going.

As long as he is on this dialysis machine, he will be in the ICU. As soon as they are comfortable enough with his progression, they will move him across the hall to intermediate care. They said it may be as soon as the end of this week! Woohoo!

Right now, Thao is either sleeping or watching movies (or taking Tylenol). When he's on dialysis, he's very cold, because his blood is exposed to room temperature for a while before it goes back in to his body. It's literally chilling to the bone. He has what's called a "bear hugger" on, which is a blanket that has air pockets. A machine blows really warm air into the pockets, and it heats him up. Needless to say, he loves it! I think as soon as he's taken off the machine, he'll be able to come out from under the blanket and use some of the gifts he got from all his friends. He's only opened a few presents because they are bargaining chips for taking Tylenol. I hope that doesn't sound too cruel, but you don't even know how stubborn this kid is. After over an hour of trying to get him to take three chewables, we believed he had finished them, only to find out after he had fallen asleep that they were still in his mouth. He was sleeping with his mouth closed, and I could hear gurgling in the back of his throat. Then I noticed he was drooling Tylenol! He had us completely fooled! It was good to see some feistiness come out when he was fighting us off, although it was frustrating.

If you guys could be praying for anything, it would be that he would continue to take his Tylenol, or that we would continue to come up with creative ways to get him to take it.

Also, some of you know that when you lie on your back for extended periods of time, your lungs will have a tendency to get lazy and close up a little. Thao's at that point right now. He taking really shallow, fast breaths. He really needs to exercise them and take deeper breaths so his oxygen level will stay up and he will be able to rest peacefully through the night. Please pray that his lungs will open up and bring some relief.

There is also a risk of infection that's always present. I have been continually praying that there would be a peace that fills this room. It's cool to hear the nurses drop little comments about the worship music or about God's bigger plan. We're surrounded by Him. Thank you for your faithfulness, love, prayers, and for being a light in dark times. It's Christ being lived out, that's what it's all about. Love you all.

—Jeff

December 14, 2011

The doctor came in to check on Thao and found that he is pretty swollen. They changed the machine today to not take off as much fluid, but they added blood as well. He ended up being 500 units "fuller." If your body can't get rid of fluid, it goes to the tissue and organs. So he is pretty swollen. This is why he's having trouble breathing. They took x-rays and found his lungs have fluid in them. Later in the day, they increased dialysis to take off more fluid than was set this morning and put him on a stronger oxygen machine that will help remove some of the fluid as well, but without drying him out. Right now, he's cold. I keep praying that God will warm him through His spirit. He's resting peacefully now.

Then Jesus said to them, "Suppose you have a friend, and you go to him at midnight and say, 'Friend, lend me three loaves of bread; a friend of mine on a journey has come to me, and I have no food to offer him.' And suppose the one inside answers, 'Don't bother me. The door is already locked, and my children and I are in bed. I can't get up and give you anything.' I tell you, even though he will not get up and give you the bread because of friendship, yet because of your shameless audacity, he will surely get up and give you as much as you need.

"So I say to you: Ask and it will be given to you; seek and you will find; knock and the door will be opened to you. For everyone who asks receives; the one who seeks finds; and to the one who knocks, the door will be opened.

"Which of you fathers, if your son asks for a fish, will give him a snake instead? Or if he asks for an egg, will give him a scorpion? If you then, though you are evil, know how to give good gifts to your children, how much more will your Father in heaven give the Holy Spirit to those who ask him!" (Luke 11:5-13)

His answer just isn't any little thing. It's His spirit. His spirit will calm Thao and warm him and heal him. Rest peacefully tonight, y'all.

—Jeff

December 15, 2011

I have a lot for you tonight. Sorry it's been getting later and later, but it's just been kinda crazy. Our kidney doctor started out the day by saying they are keeping Thao on dialysis for another full day to take more of the fluid off. Right now, they are taking off as much as his blood pressure will handle, and he's doing great. His vitals have all been good. Hemoglobin is up; calcium is up; phosphorous is being controlled. Platelets are at nineteen. He stayed off his blood pressure medicine, so he had a chance to eat, but he wasn't hungry. They are giving him Tylenol rectally now so there's no fight. He's getting full doses, so his fevers are down and he's not so cold. He still has some fluid in his lungs, so he's on more forced oxygen, though they just discussed weaning him from it. He's peeing like crazy! Up and up everyday! Our doctor is really happy. I wish you could meet this guy.

Tonight, his belly was still pretty hard and swollen, so they decided to do an ultrasound. They looked specifically at his gallbladder because of some high bilirubin. Apparently, he has a buildup of bile that has turned to sludge in there. They have to take him tomorrow to put a drain in. The good news is that it isn't backed up to his liver. The bad news is that he finally has an appetite, and before I knew better, I had Tiffany on the phone trying to get him a cheese pizza—all to find out he can't eat because of his gallbladder. Made me cry.

He's comfortable now, though. Sleeping. He doesn't complain at all, not even about his swollen body, strained breathing, catheter, rectal Tylenol, oxygen in his nose, not being able to eat when he's hungry—nothing. He's so strong. He's so big. I'm such a wuss. Nothing new. Please, just pray for him all around. I'm also aware of all the unspoken risks of taking even simple medicines, let alone the stronger ones. I'm very easily overcome with fear for the unknown. God's bigger than all that, and I believe His mission is restoration, especially in the toughest, hardest, most difficult, "all hope is lost" moments because He wants all of it. Then no one can deny His handiwork.

Prayer Requests

- ☐ Peace in His room
- ☐ That we can be a light to the doctors and nurses
- ☐ That Thao will be comforted and satisfied beyond what any food could do
- ☐ That everyone else in our family would stay healthy
- ☐ That Ava would be able to sleep peacefully through all of this change. She's having a hard time.
- ☐ For a safe, inexpensive place for our family to stay and sprawl out a little.
- ☐ For a miraculous healing of Thao's gallbladder.
- ☐ For protection from adverse side effects.
- ☐ For Mama

I don't know how to keep saying it without sounding redundant, but we are sooo thankful for you, your prayers, and your support. Love you all.

I believe; Jesus, help my unbelief. Good night.

December 15, 2011

The surgeon team made early rounds today and told us that there is no need to do surgery or a drain as of right now. They are going to keep an eye on Thao's levels and treat with meds to rid the gallbladder of the sludge. Basically, what happened is all the blood cells that had died from being jammed in the kidney finally were making their way through, and the gallbladder couldn't handle it. It's actually common of HUS, but our doctor forgot to tell us that he would be looking for that. With that, his pancreas is inflamed, because they both share the same drain. The best treatment is clear fluids and time, and it will all pass.

Thao's urine output doubled in twenty-four hours. He didn't have as much today as the day before, but he also doesn't have as much fluid in his body. The machine is also pulling off more, so the doctor isn't concerned. He wanted to take him off the machine tonight to try to "challenge" his kidneys. The physician who oversees Thao's care asked if he could wait till morning, when there were fresh people on the clock and they were ready for it. So, early tomorrow, they're going to see what his kidneys can do. The cool thing about all of this is that our doctor doesn't want to treat something that might not actually be a problem. He's not to quick to rule this as a disease that can't be worked out on dialysis alone. His other option would be to do a plasma transfer, but it has its own risks. Since he's seen regular improvement, he wants to see how much further this treatment plan will go.

Today was a rough day with the nurse, but I can't complain. I'm sure there's a lesson somewhere in there. He sat up today, though not very excited or warm; it was really cute to see him sitting up in a big chair, even. He did have a cute little scowl on his face that the doctors and nurses ate up. Thao, of course, was not excited, but it's over. I just wish they would have waited until he was off the machine because of how cold he is without his big, warm blanket. Hopefully, after he's off the machine, he will want to color in all of those cool coloring books he got from his friends.

As for what everyone has done for us, I simply cannot thank you enough. It's been great to see friends that I don't get to see very often, and especially at a time like this. Especially friends with whom you can just pick up right where you left off. We are extremely blessed.

Please continue to pray for the people who around us who are struggling through some of the same stuff. It's weird knowing that you have a pretty bad situation, but being able to look through the window between the rooms and see stuff that makes you say, "I can't imagine going through that." I just hope that these people will have the opportunity to experience the peace that comes with walking and falling dependent on Christ. A friend and I were talking about this today. I cannot imagine going through these situations without the True Hope. I would be in knots. It's hard not to be in knots when the shockers hit, even with Christ. Though He constantly proves Himself good and faithful. Amazing that it always falls back to such simple truths. Loving, truthful, faithful, merciful, forgiving, intimate, patient, good.

I started my day reading this passage this morning, John 10:10-18:

"The thief comes only to steal and kill and destroy; I have come that they may have life, and have it to the full."

"I am the good shepherd. The good shepherd lays down his life for the sheep. The hired hand is not the shepherd and does not own the sheep. So when he sees the wolf coming, he abandons the sheep and runs away. Then the wolf attacks the flock and scatters it. The man runs away because he is a hired hand and cares nothing for the sheep.

"I am the good shepherd; I know my sheep and my sheep know me— just as the Father knows me and I know the Father—and I lay down my life for the sheep. I have other sheep that are not of this sheep pen. I must bring them also. They too will listen to my voice, and there shall be one flock and one shepherd. The reason my Father loves me is that I lay down my life—only to take it up again. No one takes it from me, but I lay it down of my own accord. I have authority to lay it down and authority to take it up again. This command I received from my Father."

All to be with me.

I didn't mean to make it sound like we had no place to stay in Peoria. We needed something very specific, and after we realized what were actually asking for, we were finding that we were asking a lot. So what does God do? Gives us exactly what we need, and beyond that: an apartment with three bedrooms, large bathroom, living room with gas log, dining room, kitchen with stacked washer/dryer, office, and the kickers: one mile away, if not less, furnished, no reservation, no down payment, faith-based gift cost, and connected to downtown food bank that doesn't know what to do with all the extra food they receive week to week.

Tell me that ain't my God!

Love you all, night.

December 16, 2011

Please pray for Thao's fevers. We don't know what is causing them.

Today was the first day at the new apartment, and what a blessing it is! Liam and Ava got to stay there all day except when Ava came to see her Bubby. She really misses him and keeps saying she needs her Bubby to sleep with.

I can't explain the peace and presence.

December 18, 2011

Seized again. Fluid pull off is slow. Please pray that there are no neurological issues. Please pray for no more seizures.

No brain swelling. There is fluid but no permanent damage. It can be removed. We continue dialysis. We'll see how he is though the night and tomorrow. Thank God for the promise of His enduring love that we have to hold on to.

I want to make sure you all know that we are in no way trying to be superheroes of faith. God's all we've got. I promise you that this is not in our own strength.

Jesus answered, "Everyone who drinks this water will be thirsty again, but whoever drinks of the water that I will give them will never thirst. Indeed, the water I give them will become in them a spring of water welling up to eternal life." (John 4:13)

December 18, 2011

He's still on dialysis and should be for the next few days. His white blood cell count is down even from yesterday. It's been trending down, though they are not overly concerned right now. There are some other things that the hematologist is looking into for why his numbers have been this way. They are going to draw bone marrow and get a spinal when his platelets are high enough that it's not dangerous. They are also looking at his lymph nodes.

Looking at doing a CT scan of his chest and belly to check for malignancy.

Physical therapy is coming today to help him move a little, but he's out cold. They have him on some meds to keep his body activity down so they can get good read on his EEG. We're still waiting to talk to the neurologist.

His bilirubin and lipase are down, which means his gallbladder and pancreas are going down to normal levels. Surgery said that it would take quite awhile for it to go down. Doctors said it was the medicine, but then the resident told her we had stopped the Actigall because it was an oral med. She was puzzled. But we know why.

Thank you for your prayers. They are being answered! God continues to show Himself in so many ways. There are a lot of things that could have gone wrong yesterday. Please continue to pray for healing and for God to be seen in all of it. That everything would be for His glory.

December 19, 2011

Today was a good day. It was a busy day. The attention that we focused on Thao this weekend took away from any extra time we may have had with Ava and Liam. Tiffany and I tried to spend a few extra moments with them to help fill that need. Thao was so much more responsive today; it was fantastic. He was talking a lot more instead of just shaking or nodding his head. They took him off the EEG fairly early today because they had seen no sign of seizure activity over the twenty-four-hour period. They are keeping him on Dilantin until his kidneys begin to regulate a little better. It's not their first choice, but it's the fastest-working, which is why they are using it. We asked if we could wean him from it or switch to another, but they said they want to wait to make sure he doesn't seize again. They have reduced the dosage, so he is much more aware.

Platelets are up, hemoglobin is the same, white blood cell went up a little, lipase went up, so that is still some inflammation in the pancreas. Rest from solid food and more fluids should help. They are bypassing his pancreas with his fatty foods. His machine clotted in the middle of the night, so this time, he got hooked up with one that has a warmer. We also feel like we can control his fevers better. Though we still have a nurse or two who would like to give him Tylenol every time he sneezes. He looks better already. Less swollen in the face, hand, and feet. He's acting better, too.

After dialysis, they will do the bone marrow draw, MRI, CT scan all in a row because they can sedate him and get it all done at once. He isn't in a lot of pain, mostly irritated from all the stuff he's hooked up to. He's still peeing, but not as much.

Pray for no more seizures, less irritation, warmth, his digestive tract, kidney function. Don't stop praying for a miracle. Pray for the rest of the family and for everyone traveling to help with the kids. Pray for Tiffany and I to remember God's promise and hope and to not fear.

We've also been praying that God would bless all of you through the love and sacrifice you have shown. God's promises throughout scripture prove overabundance for the kind of love that you have shown for us.

He's sleeping now. I'm slowly learning this is when I should be sleeping, too.

—Jeff

December 21, 2011

They have confirmed through bone marrow biopsy that he indeed has HLH syndrome. We began treatments today. There are still a lot of questions, but we have been heard. God has us here for a reason for sure, and Thao is in good hands. Thank you for all of your prayers. Please continue to pray for the situation, especially all of the unknowns. Thao may have the only situation involving HLH and HUS. I know that there are people who have ideas, but please be patient with us as we work with the doctors to find the best way to approach this.

Love you all.

December 22, 2011

I'm going to try to explain some of this from how the day started and ended yesterday and what we have now for today. The doctors began yesterday intubating Thao so they could do the bone marrow biopsy and MRI. For the bone marrow, they did the biopsy in his hips at about 1:00 p.m. We had a meeting with some of the doctors and specialists about the possibility of moving toward treatment right away with at least steroids, as they had enough information to begin moving that direction. Some of our questions had to do with the fact that if they suppress his immune system with these treatments, how will we know if there is an underlying cause? Our doctors were ruling out any other cause because all bacterial tests were coming back negative, but I had questions about whether there could be any fungal problems, since those don't show up as bacteria. Two days ago (part of my meltdown), I was trying to talk to the doctors about the fact that we had been treating him for candida two weeks before all of this happened. The doctors were trying to figure out how HLH could be connected to HUS; could one cause the other, or vice versa. They were telling us that both could be caused by infection or bacteria, but again, they were ruling that out, because tests were coming back negative.

Tuesday was my day of trying to take things into my own hands. I was sitting next to Thao and had a chance to read my Bible, but instead, I googled stuff. Bad idea. It was right after they said that his pancreas enzymes went back up, so I started looking for reasons why. Then they did an ultrasound to check his pancreas, and I prayed that he wouldn't be inflamed and that the swelling would be down and there would be no other problems with it. So, sure enough, the doctor was surprised to find that nothing stood out on the ultrasound and ordered his pancreas be checked when they ran the CT scan. So God answers my prayer, and what did I do? I went and googled why his lipase would be high while his pancreas showed no signs of problems. Get that? I prayed God would heal that part, God comes through, and I doubt—taking it into my own hands, as if I could obtain the knowledge needed to fix this. The day progressed that way until I finally broke down at the end of the day, frustrated and confused and realizing that if wisdom was going to come from somewhere, it wasn't going to come from me and maybe not even from the doctors, but from God. I committed right there to leave it in His hands and to let go of the fear that drove me all day.

With that, on Wednesday, I wasn't going to fight anything or jam any information down the throat of anyone else. I would let my fears subside and let God take it into His hands. If the doctors were going to need to know something, it was going to be in His timing and instigated by Him. I decided to begin praying for God to motivate people and orchestrate the day, as He is the Great Physician.

So we ended the meeting, and they took the bone marrow. Right away, we could see the concern on the doctor's faces. They told us that they wanted to treat right away with high-dose steroids and chemo drugs to suppress the disease and that we would need to sign a consent to the treatment. They were able to get the very confirmation that they needed to diagnose him with the HLH from the bone marrow. With that, we got to meet with the hematologist, and he explained what they found and what the risks are.

There's a hospital in Cincinnati that specializes in this disease. They had been sending all of his bloodwork to them, and he had been talking regularly with the head of the department over there. That doctor was very concerned that he had already seized and was worried that it could be in his spinal fluid and possibly in his brain. They were worried about giving him a spinal tap because of his low platelet count and the risk of bleeding. The doctor in Cinci said he didn't have a choice. The risk of waiting was higher than the risk of the spinal. Our hematologist spoke with the attending physician, and they decided to add frozen plasma and platelets and within a small timeframe do the spinal and hope that the platelets would cover it.

After we signed, he asked if we had any more questions, and I told him calmly about the candida and our concern with him being septic from a fungal disease rather than a bacterial disease and maybe they were overlooking something. He became very interested and said that antifungals are a part of the treatment process for that very reason. He opened the manual and showed it to us. He asked if we had discussed it with the doctors, and after I told him yes, he asked, "Are you sure?" He said that he was going to start screening for fungus and immediately put him on an antifungal. He said he was also going to have his marrow tested for it too. He made notes, and today, we get a follow-up with all of the doctors and specialists together. Please pray for this meeting and for wisdom and for God to orchestrate all of this.

Thao still has his tube in, which is really hard to watch, but he's sedated. No tests, as far as we know today. They are going to keep him on dialysis as much as possible because of all of the added medications and treatments. Sounds like it's not only giving his kidneys a break but also his liver, because the dialysis is filtering a lot. I need to go, but I'll keep everyone posted. Thanks again for your support and prayer.

—Jeff

December 24, 2011

We thought today was going to be a day of weaning from the vent, but because of Thao's fluid overload, they have had to keep him on it. We learned tonight that it's ARDS, inflammation caused by all of the blood products added to his little body. He hasn't been able to keep his oxygen up most of the day, so tonight, they gave him a paralytic and sedated him in order to breathe for him and help remove extra fluid. We don't know how long they will be doing this. ARDS alone is a lot to cure. I already know what a lot of you are thinking and will be saying. We're here, and I'm pretty sure we aren't going to be able to go anywhere else. Please let me trust in a God that is bigger and stronger and who longs to make Himself known, *especially* when there is no hope. Please just pray for God's work, healing, restoration, and His peace and His grace that will carry us. Good night.

December 25, 2011

They are going to test Thao for some even more rare infectious diseases. So far, he's tested negative for everything he's been tested for. The doctors are going to continue with the antifungal every other day so not to add to his kidney problems. Pray that God purifies his blood.

Thao is still on dialysis and will continue to be. He's on a ventilator, and if he doesn't improve, they will put him on an oscillator vent, which is more intensive. Pray that his lactic acid goes down in his blood and his lungs clear and begin working on their own. Pray that God heals his lungs.

His lipase is still high, which means his pancreas is still overreacting and is irritated. His triglycerides are also high. With his pancreas in bad shape, they cannot give him the right food he needs to help with calories. With his triglycerides high, they are only able to give him lipids twice a week, and that's the only source of higher calories. Pray that God heals his pancreas.

He has no urine output and irritated kidneys, although the inflammatory markers are coming down. Pray that God heals his kidneys.

Please continue to pray for God's comfort and closeness to Thao as he is going through this. Pray for God's warmth, for His nourishment and satisfaction, for His gentle hand and strong protective embrace. Pray for His peace and presence in this room.

Pray for the doctors and nurses to have wisdom and skill. G'night.

Merry Christmas.

God reveals Himself in so many ways. Of all of the thing that could go wrong, He's still sustaining life. Thank you for your prayers.

December 26, 2011

They have tried changing some things on the vent to help Thao's oxygen. They believe they have found the best setting, but it's not enough. They don't want to keep "beating up" his lungs while they need to heal. The doctors have told us unless something happens between now and twelve, they are going to move Thao to ECMO life support for his lungs. Pray for God to heal his lungs.

There are doctors canceling vacations and checking on Thao from their home computers, on nights off or while out of town with family. We get many hugs throughout our days. God has blessed us with some incredible caring and skilled people. Please keep them in your prayers and ask for God's guidance and wisdom. It is amazing to hear some of these doctors who normally can fix about anybody say that they may know a lot, but there are many things they just have to leave in God's hands. The director of the PICU said that to us last night. God is present and moving. God is healing and sustaining and comforting. There is no doubt His fingerprints are all over this, but my proud self would just like to know the bigger plan. I have to rest in His sovereignty and not in my own understanding. A friend sent me a book that I haven't had time to read, but it's written from verses in Habakkuk.

God is our strength and salvation. We're not the first people to go through a difficult time. There is one truth that will remain. He is our strength and our salvation.

Habakkuk 3:17–19: "Though the fig tree should no blossom, nor fruit be on the vines, the produce of the olive fail and the fields yield no food, the flock be cut off from the fold and there be no herd in the stalls, yet I will rejoice in the LORD; I will take joy in the God of my salvation. GOD, the Lord, is my strength; he makes my feet like the deer's; he make me tread on my high places."

December 27, 2011

The bronchoscope went well today. He's swollen but not damaged. They were able to suck out some extra fluid that was in his lungs. Our doctor came in on his day off to do the procedure. He said that healing will just take some time.

The kidney dialysis machine and ECMO are battling each other for pressure and ECMO is winning. The dialysis machine went down twice today. They decided to try one more time before giving ECMO full kidney function along with the lung function. The machine can actually do lung, heart, and kidney functions at the same time, but not many of the nurses have experience with the kidney side of it.

The hematologist came in and told us this afternoon that he's not happy with the results from the first bit of treatments that he's had for HLH. The problem is that they are only able to give him 25 percent of the normal dosage because it could be toxic for his kidneys, since they are not functioning at all. He said that they are going to increase the steroids since they cannot increase the chemo dosage.

I don't know if I've explained this much, but I might as well go again. His kidneys and lungs are inflamed, and they don't know why. It's either the HLH and the inflammatory response issue, or it's a viral, bacterial, or fungal issue. The latter has been mostly ruled out, though watched, because every single lab that has been taken has come back negative. So they have to treat the HLH to try to get his lungs and kidneys to relax and heal, but they can't treat the HLH the way they need to because of his kidney issues. It's kind of a catch-22. As for right now, it sounds like the priority is HLH, lungs, then kidneys. I'm pretty sure they would take anything they could get, though. I know I will.

He's very sedated. Sleeps a lot, but we've been reading to him when we think he's awake. This morning, he was responding to me by moving his fingers. Different doctors are still commenting about how strong he is. They talk about it every night. I keep telling them that I wish they would have known Thao before all of this. Some doctors know that there is something more to this kid. Everybody who walks by the room can see that. It certainly is a lot to take in, and it has opened up some incredible discussion about what keeps us going. There's a lot of hurt up here and a lot of people searching. God's doing stuff. It's awesome to see.

I'm going to go to bed. Thank you for taking so much time of your busy lives to care, even for a moment, for Thao and pray for him. I can't thank you enough. Thank you, thank you, thank you. God's still doing something. I wish I knew what, but He's faithful all the way. We just miss our Thao. If you get a chance and you want to know a little more about this kid, you can start by reading past entries of my wife's blog. It's enlightening, for sure. We just sat and talked for about a half an hour about some great memories that aren't at all that far back. Anyway. Love you guys. I just talked to another father tonight whose son's heart is failing and they don't know why. Pray that we would continue to have opportunities to talk with some of the other people up here. There's an incredible amount of openness. Anyway, really, good night.

-Jeff

December 29, 2011

I'm starting this update without really knowing where I'm going. I hope it's not too confusing. We just have a lot on our minds and no good way of explaining it.

The last couple of days have been pretty calm and quiet. There have not been any new developments. ECMO is doing its job, and so is the dialysis machine. The nurses are running around trying to keep all of the IVs going and dealing with the dialysis machine, checking on him, sucking the fluid out of his lungs, doing bloodwork, checking his blood gasses, and filling out all of the paperwork that goes along with it. He's been pretty well sedated so that he doesn't throw the ECMO machine off, which can easily be done by even a slight movement of his head. When he does wake up (we can usually tell by his heart rate going up), we have been reading to him. We've read *The Mouse and the Motorcycle, Ralph S. Mouse, The Lion, the Witch and the Wardrobe, The Magician's Nephew,* and the best children's Bible out there, *The Jesus Storybook Bible.* It's amazing how the *Chronicles of Narnia* books and the children's Bible can be such an awesome reminder of our God and His infinite love for us. Yes, that would be Tiffany and I. When Aslan sacrifices himself in all of his glory for Edmund, and then Lucy and Susan had lost all hope because Aslan had died, but then Aslan came back to life and smashed the Stone Table, yeah, there were tears.

The hematologist spoke with Tiffany two nights ago and said that he was really upset about the results of the treatment. Basically, it wasn't doing anything. The two machines that oxygenize his blood and put his kidneys through dialysis have really good filters on them. Great for his body, not so great for the medications. They have decided to double the recommended steroid dosage and continued on with the chemo treatments. They had only done one last week. Then we spoke last night, and he tried to explain some more of what was going on. Basically, they're not sure if there is still some infection in the background or not. All of his tests have come back negative, but that's not necessarily a good thing. He said the tests are not accurate; they're sensitive. Basically, that means that if the tests find an infection, they can pinpoint it, but if it doesn't come back positive, it doesn't mean it's not there. That goes for the fungal tests too. So they're not sure if he's inflamed because of infection or from the blood disorder. He said they could use stronger drugs to kill his lymphosites, but those might be the only cells holding the infection at bay. That is, if there is an infection. He also said that the lungs have really slowed everything down, probably because of ECMO.

I asked him some questions about side effects to different shots he's had (immunization and such), and he said that one of the causes of HLH is actually immunizations. Well, that got Tiffany's wheels spinning, and she spent about an hour and a half on google looking at different things like mercury or lead poisoning, two tests they had not done yet. Thao has reacted to his immunizations every single time he's had one, and it's always gotten worse after each one. Awhile ago, we even decided not to give him all the immunizations because of the high risk. Then we also found the Rocephin shot he got the Monday before all of this has some pretty severe side effects like kidney disease, lung disease, pancreatitis, sludge in the gallbladder, and red blood cells being attacked from his own system … hmmmmmm … sounds a little too close to home. Tiffany got a chance to talk to one of our doctors about it tonight, and he was extremely attentive to it. They ran the mercury and lead tests today, and we'll find out more tomorrow.

Right now, every problem is preventing the other problem from being resolved. They can't fully treat the HLH because the treatment could be toxic to what's left of his kidneys; they can't do anything until his lungs are healed because ECMO is clearing everything out; and his kidneys are on the back burner, even though both are held back because they are inflamed by something else that can't be treated until his organs are better. Did you get all of that? Neither did I. Our hematologist asked if I had any more questions, and I laughed and said I had about a thousand but I can't wrap my head around it right now.

We are speaking with other people who are a little bit outside the box, and maybe I can talk more about that tomorrow.

For right now, Thao is not getting the nutrition that his body needs. We thought that with the pancreas levels decreasing, they would consider using the feeding tube again, but they can't because one of the blood pressure medicines he's on constricts blood to his bowels, thereby making it difficult for him digest anything at all. He's lost a lot of weight. We keep asking him if he hurts and he shakes his head no, so that is good. I think he might be uncomfortable, but at least he has that air mattress instead of the normal hospital beds. Otherwise, we'd be dealing with bedsores too. He's still here. He's still very, very handsome. Then nurses keep saying he's beautiful, and I would have to agree, but someday he might read this and get mad at me, so I'll stick with handsome. He's still so strong, and we keep telling him how proud we are of him. He's certainly a fighter. We miss him a lot, and we sure can't wait to hold him again. We can't wait to hear him say, "Love you," or shoot a quick wink at us, or to hear his dinosaur roar with a following giggle. I don't think we too often took life for granted, but it sure makes us think about all that we have. We have certainly been blessed. And we are continually being blessed by God through all of you. Sorry for not posting earlier. I know there are a lot of people eager and ready to pray for us, and I thank you so much for that. Some days are harder than others to have something ready to say, to even want to dive into it. It's awesome, though, because even when fear or doubt slips in, God seems to remind us in very simple ways (like reading his children's stories) that He's here and He loves and He hears every cry. He's our hope, our salvation, our comfort and peace. I think I'm going to bed. Love you all.

—Jeff

December 30, 2011

Count it all joy my brothers when you meet trials of various kinds. For you know that the testing of your faith produces steadfastness. And let steadfastness have its way that you may be perfect and complete, not lacking in anything. (James 1:2-4)

December 31, 2011

We need some prayer for wisdom and peace tonight. Things have been relatively low-key the last five days since he's been on ECMO.

He isn't necessarily getting worse, but he's not getting better either. The hematologist is ready to use another treatment that they would normally use in a bone marrow transplant. It is supposed to wipe out all of his lymphocites. If there is still an underlying infection, this is the only thing that is keeping the infection at bay. Because all of his viral, bacterial, and fungal tests keep coming back negative (tested by DNA, antibodies produced, and by cultures; they cannot go by the antibodies, but all tests came back negative by way of the other two testing methods), they are assuming that the inflammation in his kidneys, lungs, pancreas, etc., is caused by the HLH. So by knocking the lymphocites out, they would be taking care of the HLH problem, but if HLH is not the problem and an underlying infection that might be under radar is causing the inflammation, he will be overtaken by the infection for lack of an immune system. They wanted Tiffany and I to decide tonight, but we are obviously in no rush on this decision. We wanted at least tonight to pray about it, and we told them we would have an answer by tomorrow morning. If ever Thao needed prayer, it's tonight. Please, make phone calls or whatever you have to, to encourage people to pray. It's the new year, and everyone is up late anyway. Let's pray all night. Pray for the inflammation to go down all over his body. Pray for complete healing of any viral, bacterial, or fungal infection. Pray for his kidneys, liver, and pancreas to be miraculously healed. Pray for his blood to be purified. Pray for his rest, comfort, and peace. Pray for God to move, restore, and revive.

Pray that God would be made known tonight; that He would glorify Himself in the middle of this calamity.

January 1, 2012

This morning, we asked the doctor if we would be able to talk to the whole team of people involved with the care and treatment of Thao. She said that she would be more than happy to arrange it. She got everyone together to present the situation with the other doctors first. So everyone was making phone calls and meeting in the room from 9:30 until Tiffany and I were able to meet with them at 1:30 p.m. We knew most of what was on their minds concerning the treatment and what they wanted to do. This meeting was mostly for our questions. They expressed how much they liked us asking questions and doing our own research outside of their assessments of the situation. They thoroughly answered our questions, and we have concluded that the treatment that they recommend is the best direction in which to head. Now, there are many risks to doing the treatment, as I had stated in the last post, but at this point, time is one of the most important aspects of his recovery.

We could wait to see if his lungs recover without treating the HLH, but we don't necessarily have two weeks to find out. If we get to that point and then realize that HLH is the issue, then we are very far behind for lung and kidney recovery. We are already midway of week three out of the twelve weeks we have to recover his kidneys. Again, kidneys are usually the first organs to go and the last to recover, so we need as much time as possible, especially if HLH is causing the inflammation that is preventing healing for his kidneys.

Obviously, with wiping out his lymphocites, our biggest concern is that there might still be some underlying infection in his bloodstream. The doctors have tested and treated for everything that it could be, including many rare infectious diseases. There are thousands of other diseases that each require specific treatment, and there is no way they could possibly treat for everything, especially when most of those treatments have pretty harsh consequences to the body.

This has been the most difficult decision of our lives. Please, if you have an opinion about the choice that we made, I would ask kindly for you to keep it to yourself. I spoke over the phone with the director of the ICU today, and he remarked that Thao is the sickest kid on this floor and probably the sickest child he's treated in many years. Right now, there are no right answers. If we withhold treatment, he has just as much risk for a full recovery. If his lungs do not heal in a given amount of time, they will not last and he will need new. If his kidneys do not heal in a given amount of time, they will not last and he will need new. If he gets new kidneys, there is no chance of him getting a bone marrow transplant that he most definitely needs at the end of the HLH treatment (months down the road). I recognize that with being so transparent in our situation, we run the risk of becoming vulnerable to accusation and "this is what you should have done or what you should do now" statements.

If I can, I would like to make my appeal to you. Last night, after posting, I had an awesome time of worship and prayer with Thao. We went for a couple of hours, and then I fell asleep and woke up to Kurt and Kimberly Sovine waiting in the lobby. I went out and had an awesome conversation with them about God's grace for each of us in every tough spot we might find ourselves in. I hear a lot people say that they can't imagine being in our position. The cool thing is that you don't have to. Through all of this, we've gotten to experience God's grace and peace in a way that I could never explain to you. I think of where Thao's at because he is the one who has to go through all of it, but I believe that Thao's getting to experience the love and comfort and power of God in a way that only he has the opportunity to experience.

There are people all over the world who have been in a similar situation in having a sick child. There are people at the southern tip of Africa that are literally watching family members waste away to nothing for lack of food and water, and you know what? I believe God hears their cries and weeps with them. He doesn't promise that he's going to fix everything we want when we want it. Just after Jesus fed that huge crowd with a single meal in John 6, the crowd wanted to make him king of Israel. Jesus got away because the way he was going to reign was very different than what the Jews had in mind. They finally found him across the sea the next day, and Jesus answered them:

"Very truly I tell you, you are looking for me, not because you saw the signs I performed but because you ate the loaves and had your fill. Do not work for food that spoils, but for food that endures to eternal life, which the Son of Man will give you. For on him God the Father has placed his seal of approval." (John 6:26-27)

The Jews were expectant of a very physical king and kingdom that they, though, would reign in a militaristic way, with borders and all. All other countries to bow to the nation of Israel, and this king was going to reign forever, and their kingdom would trump all other kingdoms. They saw Jesus's feeding as prophecy come true; this was who they were waiting for. Jesus explained to them that the food that he has is eternal, and the crowd asked how they could get some of that food (still thinking physical).

Then Jesus declared, "I am the bread of life. Whoever comes to me will never go hungry, and whoever believes in me will never be thirsty. But as I told you, you have seen me and still you do not believe. All those the Father gives me will come to me, and whoever comes to me I will never drive away. For I have come down from heaven not to do my will but to do the will of him who sent me. And this is the will of him who sent me, that I shall lose none of all those he has given me, but raise them up at the last day. For my Father's will is that everyone who looks to the Son and believes in him shall have eternal life, and I will raise them up at the last day." (John 6:35-40)

The bread He speaks of is his presence. He promises Himself and his eternal kingdom. My Uncle Mark told me that the word *peace* is derived from a Hebrew word that means, "all debts paid".

Reminds me of the passage in Colossians: "Set your hearts on things above where Christ is seated at the right hand of God, set your minds on things above, not on earthly things. For you died and your life is hid with Christ in God. When Christ who is your life appears you will appear with Him in Glory."

So what am I getting at now that you've been reading for the last half hour?

You know what God told me last night? *Trust me.*

You know what He told Tiffany? *Trust me.*

What, then, shall we say to these things? If God is for us, who can be against us? He who did not spare his own Son but gave him up for us all, how will he not also with him graciously give us all things? Who shall bring any charge against God's elect? It is God who justifies. Who is to condemn? Christ Jesus is the one who died—more than that, who was raised—who is at the right hand of God, who indeed is interceding for us. Who shall separate us from the love of Christ? Shall tribulation, or distress, or persecution, or famine, or nakedness, or danger, or sword? As it is written, "For your sake we are being killed all the day long; we are regarded as sheep to be slaughtered. No, in all these things, we are more than conquerors through him who loved us. For I am sure that neither death nor life, nor angels nor rulers, nor things present nor things to come, nor powers, nor height nor depth, nor anything else in all creation, will be able to separate us from the love of God in Christ Jesus our Lord. (Romans 8:31-39)

That's my God and my peace.

Good night.

January 3, 2012

Today at 3:00, our attending physician and hematologist stopped me in the hallway and said they had just been talking about Thao. They told me to have a seat. At this point, Tiffany and I had told them that we would do the treatment, but it never was quite official as far as signing paperwork and such. We were both okay that no one had approached us with paperwork quite yet. They hadn't really seemed like they were in too big of a rush (odd), but again, we were okay with that. I thought this was them wanting confirmation and to have us sign some papers. I was wrong.

Earlier in the day, we had seen an x-ray of his lungs that looked night and day different, and quite honestly, it shouldn't have looked that good, because they had done absolutely nothing to recruit his lungs. That was part of our frustration with yesterday, that they kept saying that his lungs hadn't looked any better, but we knew they weren't going to as long as they just let them sit on the "low setting" of the vent. But again, this is a different doctor than the one we had this weekend. She told me that not only did the lungs look better, but that his numbers all looked good. When they started him on ECMO, he was on full support, 100 percent. Yesterday, he was on 50 percent. Today, they took him down to 40 percent, which means his lungs were doing 60 percent of the work, again, on low setting of the ventilator.

His blood oxygen level had been in the low to mid sixties since yesterday, and their goal was forties to fifties. She said that they are going to start recruiting or exercising his lungs tomorrow and not to get our hopes up too much, but they might be able to get him off of ECMO by the beginning of next week, or if he does really well, maybe by the end of this week.

Then she started talking about his blood pressure. He has had low blood pressure, and he's on two medications for keeping it balanced. I'm not sure how much of this is going to make sense, but just try to follow. ECMO has to have good volume in order to work. There is an alarm that goes off when he's low and they add more blood, plasma, platelets, or saline in order to get him back up to where the machine will run well. The way that they measure his volume is from the ECMO machine's bladder pressure. The pressure was showing normal, so he should have normal volume and pressure. But his pressure is usually low, and his skin's really dry, which makes him appear dry. Well, he's been dry. The bladder pressure is not giving an accurate read because of the dialysis machine being hooked up to the system. So he's actually been more negative than they thought. They caught it today and added volume through the dialysis machine, and they are going to try to keep him a little bit positive. This will also be good for his kidneys. When you're dehydrated, your kidneys try to retain as much fluid as possible, and in turn, you don't have to urinate. If they give him extra fluid, he's more likely to urinate. More likely—no guarantees.

The lungs and his blood pressure were reasons why one doctor wanted to act quickly. To her, it seemed as though these were sure-tale signs that the HLH was getting even more out of control and the treatment he was already on was not working. This made her ask our hematologist to look into other options and is the reason why we ended up in that meeting yesterday. We didn't agree with her assessment of the two situations, because we were told ahead of time about his lungs not "looking better" because they weren't being used and we also knew that ECMO could change his blood pressure with the slightest change.

Our hematologist took over at this point and said that he wanted to wait with the treatment and see if we can recruit his lungs and get him off ECMO so we will have more accurate lab work and know better whether the treatment is effective or not. His fear is that in doing the new treatment, there is no turning back. He would rather approach it more cautiously if we have the time, which we agree. He wants to wait for at least a couple of days. They are going to run the most common viruses again in his bloodwork and make sure he's clear before they treat, and they won't get results until Thursday. We have at least until Friday to see improvement. Of course, they will be assessing this constantly, but for now, that's the plan.

One other thing the two doctors discussed is that once he is off ECMO, they want to transfer him to a bone-marrow transplant facility. His first recommendation is Cincinnati, but he said he would also highly recommend Chicago. Cincinnati is the HLH treatment center. These facilities would better accommodate Thao and a suppressed immune system, because that's what they are used to.

They told me not to get too excited yet and that a lot could change, but how could I not? This is the first good report we've had in two and a half weeks, and God's fingerprints are all over it. There were more prayers answered in that twenty-minute conversation than I have time to tell you right now. Our God is *awesome*!

January 4, 2012

I woke up yesterday to a doctor, surgeon, and six nurses turning Thao over onto his stomach. Usually, at least a couple of times a night, I find myself quickly in a prayerful position begging God's protection for Thao. I think the best way that I have decided to explain Thao's situation is if you can remember back with me the old *Looney Tunes* Marvin the Martian cartoon. Most of the time, Marvin the Martian ended up destroying most of his planet except for one very, very small part that only had a little dirt and a long root coming down that he had a hold of, which was the only thing that kept him from falling into the dark vastness of space.

Anyway, this was another one of those moments where it only takes one small movement for a lot of things to go wrong. He's got so many lines running off his arms, he has a tube for the ventilator, all kinds of sensors with wires, and last but not least, two quite large tubes coming out his neck that control his largest supply of blood going to the ECMO machine (that's why the surgeon was there). The point of turning him "prone," as they call it, is to get the fluid and mucous that settles in the bottom of his lungs to be moved and to maybe give them a chance to suck it out. They did it, and I could breathe again.

It was also good for another reason. His spine was starting to get sores—thankfully, not open sores—that they weren't able to see when he was on his back. Another way that God worked in all of this is that the first week that we were here, the nurses wanted to spoil Thao and get him a bed that was a giant air mattress. Nobody knew that he wasn't going to be able to move for two and a half weeks. We have not had to deal with bedsores like we would have if he had the first bed he was in.

After that, they immediately prepared for another brachioscope. Our same doctor did it, and this time, Thao's lungs were much less swollen, and you could see how turning him onto his stomach was a really good thing. They were sucking out mucous that kept clogging the scope. They got most of it out, and the doctor said that he was very pleased with how things were looking. They decided that they wanted to move him to a different ventilator called an oscillator that is gentler on the lungs. It shoots really light jets of air into his lungs at a rate of sixty breaths a minute to keep a constant pressure in his lungs. They mostly use it on infants up here because of how gentle it is compared to the other ventilator. The first blood gas didn't look very good, but they said that it probably just needed a little bit of time to get things going.

This morning, I woke up and the nurses said, "Hey, you want to see something that will make you really happy?" His x-ray of his lungs today was amazing! If you remember, their goal for his blood gas was the forties to fifties, and he was hanging around the sixties. They showed me his blood gasses, and they were in the 130s and 140s. They said that their next step was to lessen the workload of ECMO, which is already running at 40 percent. I also want to remind you that the machines he's on don't actually heal anything. All that they can do is push his lungs, but they can't get them to respond. That's God's business. His blood gasses weren't anywhere close to that number when he was running 100 percent on ECMO, let alone now. The plan is to turn him back over onto his back.

Love you all. Thank you so much for the prayers. He's not out of the rut yet, but God is definitely doing His work. He always is.

—Jeff

January 6, 2012

We are just blown away by the number of people involved with this group, and then the updates that keep getting whole churches praying, and how incredibly we've been blessed by so many of you, both friends and people we have never met. I cannot express to you what this means to us. Don't stop praying, please. We are still in the rough of things, though it has been nice to get some good news. Every day and night, we are in the battle for his life.

The last day and a half have been okay days, but with no improvement. His lungs seem to be at a standstill, and nothing else is getting better. His liver and spleen are starting to swell, but their numbers seem to be showing that everything is functioning well. We had another meeting with the doctors today, and they said that we probably need to still consider the Campath chemo drug again. They said that if we are comfortable, they could start the treatment tomorrow, but we are not all too comfortable with it right now. We are still hopeful that his lungs could heal by Monday. If they could wait to get him off ECMO, they would be able to transfer him to another facility that is used to dealing with immuno-suppressed children. Then they could continue the treatment within a facility that is a little more controlled. We have not officially given the okay for the Campath, but we are going to tell them that we would like to wait until Monday unless anything becomes an issue between now and then.

Please pray for his lungs to heal, for his kidneys to heal and produce urine, that he will be able to come off of his blood pressure medicines so he can get a feeding tube, that his HLH treatment will *show* progress in some way, that God would purify his blood. Please continue to pray for God's presence in this room and for God to be near Thao through this time. We ran into two parents this week who spoke about things that their children experienced through their illnesses. They spoke about being comforted by Jesus and angels and that dying is okay and doesn't hurt. I'm telling you, I know God wanted me to hear that. It was confirmation that my God cares more about my child than I possibly could and that He has complete access and control. How cool is that?

Please pray for Tiffany and me. Pray that God would continue to hold onto us and that we would be moldable and used by him.

If you do a word study on humility, you will find that humility is purely dependence on God, completely falling into his grace, mercy, faith, hope, and love. Every day, we're reminded that He is all we have. Every night, too, for that matter. By God's grace, we can "count it all joy ... for the testing of your faith produces steadfastness (in Christ), that we may be perfect and complete (in Christ) not lacking in anything. There is a promise of His faithfulness, His hope, and His love."

On a side note to all of this, some friends and family set up a site that handles fundraisers for stuff like this. Please do not feel obligated. I stress that *so* much. God has been taking care of us and will continue to provide. Some people have been asking for the best way to send some money our way, and our friend went out to research the best way to make it happen. Again, many of you have already given so much, and we would really love to make sure you know how much it means that you have been so prayerful and thoughtful, even through the middle of the night. Thank you, thank you, thank you for everything. The meals have been awesome, the apartment we have been staying is awesome, and all of you are awesome.

Just pray for open doors. If someone would like to help out more, I would love to get my hands on some small Book of John Bibles. If you do send some, please send something at least a little bit reader friendly. I really like the "Hope for Today" God's Word translation. From my experience, it holds pretty closely. I would love to get some in the hands of the people here and maybe spur some conversation. There's plenty of sitting and waiting time and an amazing openness, so I figure, why not, right?

Love you all so much. Thank you, as always.

January 7, 2012

Please pray for Thao's blood pressure to go up. They are starting him on another blood pressure medicine, which would make it his third. There are obvious complications to him being on so many at once.

Also, the infectious disease doctor came in today and said that two markers that could mean fungal infection came back positive. They already upped his broad spectrum anti-fungal once, and now they're upping it again to an even stronger one until they find out more of what's going on. He also tested positive for a common Herpes-6 virus that he's already had some of with his roseola. It's called HHV-6, and it will stay in the system and reactivate. It's one that they were concerned about reactivating when they've been talking about the Campath treatment. They sent out bloodwork yesterday to California, which we won't get back until next week, that will tell how much is in his blood. The amount that's in his blood will be more telling of how long it's been in his system. If there are infections, they could be affecting his blood pressure too and obviously many more complications, since he doesn't have the best immune system to start with.

There are many more things to pray about in the post I made yesterday, in case you haven't had a chance to read it already.

Thanks again and love,

—Jeff

His blood pressure has been regulated. Now it seems like whatever infection is there is starting to have an effect on his body. He's already on a strong antibiotic and anti-fungal. You know the dril; please pray for God's presence and comfort and peace right now.

January 8, 2012

This morning in rounds, they showed his x-ray, and it's back to fluid overload. When your body gets an infection, the blood vessels will swell, thereby causing your blood pressure to go down. The blood-pressure meds correct that, constrict the blood vessels, but the problem with using too much of it is that it will constrict some places, like in the bowels, that could cause a lot of other problems. So instead of increasing the meds, they decided to give him more blood product to create more volume and bring the pressure back up. Right now, he's about two liters full. They were concerned last night with the size of his stomach region and were going to do a test to see if there was another disorder beginning but decided against it, saying that the risk wasn't worth knowing. This morning, the doctor said that it's safe to assume that it's where it is because of the amount of fluid that's in him.

As I posted before, they have him on four strong antibiotics/anti-fungals that are all broad-coverage. Yesterday, they had decided against treating him for the positive viral test that came back, because the antivirus is toxic to kidneys. Today, they have decided to go ahead with a smaller dosage treatment, just in case.

Everything else as of now remains the same. They did do an echo-cardiogram today, and his heart is functioning "really well," as quoted by the cardiologist.

There have been so many lies infiltrating my mind throughout the past day. It's so hard to wrap my head around the complete goodness and steadfast love of God sometimes—well, all the time. But I will tell you that when He's ready to reveal it, He doesn't hold back. A day before, I was asking God to use me and mold me, and the next day, I'm a heaping mess of uncertainty, anger, and frustration. Why would God …? Is He using this to teach me …? All at the expense of …? If He's angry with me, why doesn't he bring it all down on me and stop using my child?

He spoke this answer to me today:

> Jeff, "just because I work incredible good out of unspeakable tragedies doesn't mean I orchestrate the tragedies. Don't ever assume that my using something means I caused it or that I needed it to accomplish my purposes. That will only lead you

to false notions about me. Grace doesn't depend on suffering to exist, but where there is suffering, you will find grace in many facets and colors." (from *The Shack* by William P. Young)

And then I read this: "There is no fear in love, but perfect love casts out fear. For fear has to do with punishment, and whoever fears has not been perfected in love." (1 John 4:18)

It's funny how quickly I can complicate God's steadfast love. I'm slowly learning not to look so closely at the good and the bad reports. I don't want to be changed based on those things; I want to be changed because I'm walking through all of this darkness with Christ recognizing that if anyone understands the pain and torment of all of this, it's Him. And in that, there's all the grace and peace I could possibly need. I keep coming back to: "If you have been raised with Christ, set your hearts on things above where Christ is seated at the right hand of God. Set your minds on things above, not on earthly things for you died (to myself) and your life is hid with Christ in God. When Christ who is your life appears, you will appear with him in glory." (Colossians 3:1-4) That promise isn't for when I'm gone; it's for right now. God, please bring your kingdom and have your way.

January 9, 2012

I want to start by again thanking everyone for everything. It's getting redundant, but not to us. We have received so much from all of you. We're so encouraged by every way you have made your love known to us. We've had some awesome food and an incredible amount of financial support. People have been giving through the Fundly account that our friend set up for us, and people have been giving incredibly outside of that. Thank you, thank you, thank you. I can't tell you what it means to me that I don't have be back home working and separated from my family.

This morning it appeared that he was having a good response to the antibiotic/anti-fungal/anti-viruses he has been receiving. But after looking at the blood work, it didn't take long to see that there's a good chance that he is septic. Doctors are discussing putting him on ECMO for his heart as well. Right now, they are monitoring how much his blood is pumping through his heart per minute. Normal is three to four liters, and he's at ten, which means his heart is doing too much. The good thing is that they are already doing what they should be doing if he is septic. It's just a matter of what organs they will have to support through the process. They are also going to do another plasma transfer, which will help purify his blood. It consists of actually removing plasma and adding new plasma to the blood.

They did another bronchioscopy this morning, and his lungs looked good, though a little more inflamed than last time. But he didn't have as much mucous in there. All of the fluid was thin, so they were able to get a good amount for tests and cultures.

If they do move him over to ECMO, it's another surgical procedure to put a larger cath in, and they will have to run it into an artery and bypass the flow around his heart, so it's rather extensive.

That's all I have for now. I'll keep you updated if anything changes.

Love you all,
Jeff

January 10, 2012

Okay, I'll do a quick one tonight. They are starting Campath tonight at 10:30. The long-term effects of his immune system being bottomed out have to be overlooked because there is an immediate need to go after the HLH with everything at our disposal. The short-term effects, though, are allergic reactions and the chance of it lowering his blood pressure, both of which his body will most likely not handle very well. If ever we needed your prayers …

Love you all, and thank you all. So much love,

—Jeff

January 12, 2012

Thank you so much for your prayers. Sorry for the delay in updates. We just spoke with the doctors, and they said that they are out of options. We might be coming to the end. Thank you so much, all of you, for everything. We love you all so much. Please keep praying for peace in all of this.

—Jeff

January 13, 2012

Thao is with Jesus now.

Epilogue

and he is still my son.

"And as He spoke, He no longer looked to them like a lion; but the things that began to happen after that were so great and beautiful that I cannot write them. And for us this the end of all stories, and we can most truly say that they all lived happily ever after. But for them it was only the beginning of the real story. All their life in this world and all their adventures in Narnia had only been the cover and the title page: now at last they were beginning Chapter One of the Great Story which no one on earth has read: which goes on for ever: in which every chapter is better than the one before."

–From *The Last Battle* by C.S. Lewis

We have reached the end, but truly, it is not the end. My original thoughts were to allow a place for family to share their own stories and memories, because I love to hear them. I love to talk about my son. But I have decided to leave these pages blank. For those of you who knew Thao, you may choose to make this space your journal of remembering. For those of you who only knew him through this book and his story, I pray that God has lead you to a place of closeness with Him through Thao's story. I hope you have wonderful, exciting adventures to journal here. Adventures in the stillness. Adventures in knowing God more. Memories of loved ones to treasure.

But it's not really about all that, is it? Because this isn't really the end for Thao. He is with our Saviour, our Creator, our King. You can have this same hope of eternity in heaven with Christ. I pray that Jesus tugs on your heart so hard that you let Him in to change your life.